T0329964

INDUSTRIAL ECONOMICS
FOR
COUNTRIES IN TRANSITION

Industrial Economics for Countries in Transition

Evidence from Eastern Europe
and Asia Pacific

Edited by
Philippe R. Scholtès

United Nations
Industrial Development Organization

Edward Elgar
Cheltenham, UK • Northampton, MA, USA

Published by
Edward Elgar Publishing Limited
Glensanda House
Montpellier Parade
Cheltenham
Glos GL50 1UA
UK

Edward Elgar Publishing, Inc.
136 West Street
Suite 202
Northampton
Massachusetts 01060
USA

Reprinted 2002

A catalogue record for this book
is available from the British Library

Library of Congress Cataloguing in Publication Data
Industrial economics for countries in transition: evidence from
  Eastern Europe and Asia Pacific / edited by Philippe R. Scholtès.
    "United Nations Industrial Development Organization."
    Includes bibliographical references.
    1. Industrial policy. 2. Privatization—Germany (East)—Case
  studies. 3. Germany. Treuhandanstalt. 4. Industrialization-
  –Vietnam—Red River Delta. I. Scholtès, Philippe R., 1960–
  HD3611.I373 1996
  338.9—dc20   96–18297
                                                                   CIP

ISBN 978 1 85898 521 3

Printed and bound by CPI Group (UK) Ltd, Croydon, CR0 4YY

Contents

Tables

Figures

Abbreviations and Acronyms

ASEAN	Association of South-East Asian Nations
BOO	build-own-operate
BOT	build-own-transfer
CCT	core counterpart team
CKD	complete knock-down kit
CMEA	Council for Mutual Economic Assistance
DBPF	domestic best practice frontier
ECN	economic capability of a nation
EA	East Asia
EE	Eastern Europe
EPZ	export processing zone
ESCAP	Economic and Social Commission for Asia and the Pacific
ESOP	employee stock ownership plan
FDI	foreign direct investment
FTC	firm level technological capability
GATT	General Agreement on Tariffs and Trade
GNP	gross national product
GDP	gross domestic product
GRP	gross regional product
HCMC	Ho Chi Minh City
ICOR	incremental capital/output ratio
IBPF	international best practice frontier
IMF	International Monetary Fund
ISIC	International Standards of Industrial Classification
MBO	management buy-out
MERIT	Maastricht Economic Research Institute on Innovation and Technology
MVA	manufacturing value added
MOSTE	Ministry of Science, Technology and Environment, Government of Viet Nam
NEC	non-equity cooperation

NIC	newly industrialized country
NTC	national level technological capability
NTZ	Northern Triangle Zone
OECD	Organisation for Economic Co-operation and Development
ODA	Official Development Aid
RCA	revealed comparative advantage
RRD	Red River Delta region of Viet Nam
SBVN	State Bank of Viet Nam
SCCI	State Committee for Cooperation and Investment, Government of Viet Nam
SME	Small- and medium-scale enterprises
SOE	State-owned enterprise
SPC	State Planning Committee, Government of Viet Nam
SSA	stabilization and structural adjustment programme
TNC	transnational corporation
TFP	total factor productivity
UNDP	United Nations Development Programme
UNIDO	United Nations Industrial Development Organization
WTO	World Trade Organization

Foreword

There is among developing countries a growing consensus on the effectiveness of market economics to bolster growth by virtue of a more efficient allocation of resources. Indeed, it is generally reckoned that central planning approaches and heavy government intervention have failed altogether to deliver sustainable development. They have instead brought along widening budget deficits, balance-of-payment distortions and, as far as manufacturing is concerned, an uncompetitive and structurally inadequate industrial fabric.

Beyond its traditional role of purveyor of public goods – characterized by significant consumption externalities, or increasing return-to-scale – the public sector in many countries pervaded the entire productive economy, with often dismal results. It is not, as frequently stated, that civil servants necessarily make poor managers. More fundamentally, the root causes are to be found with *(a)* the ambiguous – and abuse-prone – situation of the same actor setting the rules of the game and playing by these rules, and *(b)* the weak form of a budget constraint typical of public enterprises. This unfortunate situation triggered a spiral of crowding out of domestic investment away from private initiative, poor management and industrial performances, low competitiveness, increased protection to secure domestic markets and structural distortions.

Profound economic reforms were introduced during the last decade in developing countries and in eastern Europe alike to break this vicious circle. A strong emphasis was placed on private sector development, while the State was to confine itself to setting up a conducive environment and to ensuring a fair play of market forces. Prominent among a range of instruments, large privatization programmes were initiated in an attempt to reduce budget deficits by outright divesture, and/or to let market mechanisms steer an industrial restructuring consistent with underlying comparative advantages.

xiv

Today the needs of an emerging private sector are manifold. Indeed in a market economy, its development hinges upon its capacity to strengthen, or acquire, a competitive position by means of a strategic combination of products, processes and markets. Competitiveness in turn encompasses a string of variables such as labour or capital productivity, efficiency in the selected mix of factors, corporate taxation, customs duties, cost of utilities and transportation facilities.

Thus, fostering industrial development in a newly established market set-up by all means represents a formidable challenge to the policy maker, and one for which he is seldom prepared.

The purpose of this book is to expose, in clear and practical terms, the major issues facing the public authorities in transition economies as well as, for that matter, in most developing countries at the turn of the century. While firmly grounded in mainstream industrial and development economic theory, it essentially draws from a wide body of empirical evidence to illustrate its views and support its arguments.

The book is divided into two parts: Part I is essentially of a conceptual nature, and addresses the pervasive issues of the day. Part II gives the reflection a more concrete turn, and proceeds with a field application of some of the points developed in the first part.

Part I consists of five papers altogether, arranged in a logical sequence. Chapter 1 sets the stage with a long-term perspective of industrial growth, and the necessary accumulation of technological capabilities to that end. From the observation of development patterns in East and South-East Asia it highlights the benefits of export orientation and the collective gains derived from 'selective interventionism', a critical – and controversial – issue in the developing world at large.

The overall framework of economic restructuring is analysed in Chapter 2, where the recent eastern European experiences prompt a series of lessons in terms of the concomitant reforms that must be implemented, and the pitfalls to be avoided along the process. The success of a restructuring programme will be ultimately determined by the commitment of the public authorities to its unfettered implementation, and by the social consensus cemented around transparent objectives and policies.

The scope of investigation narrows down somewhat in Chapter 3 to focus on industrial restructuring in the framework of economic reforms. Most visible among the many facets of industrial restructuring are the privatization programmes initiated in a large number of countries, across virtually the entire spectrum of development stages. The chapter illustrates the process from the identification of firms slated for privatization, the obstacles often encountered, and the practical ways and means generally applied. Yet, outright privatization is not always economically advisable, nor politically feasible. Alternative paths are successfully followed in several countries, where privatization without transfer of ownership aims at subjecting the firm's management to proxies of market signals.

Although hardly replicable to different contexts, the case of the 'Treuhandanstalt' presented in Chapter 4 is an interesting example of institutional support to industrial restructuring. Initially established as a caretaker, on behalf of the Government, of public enterprises in the former German Democratic Republic, the agency rapidly turned in its next avatar into a powerful instrument of industrial policy. In its nearly five years of existence, the Treuhandanstalt engineered the disposal of more than 12,000 enterprises through privatization, denationalization, decentralization or, in a significant number of cases, liquidation.

Chapter 5 raises the critical interrogation faced by policy makers while sailing through the rough winds of transition: what, if any, is the role of the Government in the emerging market set-up? The paper argues in favour of a considerable overhaul of public governance in general, and particularly towards building a strong capacity in the field of industrial economics. Sorely lacking in transition economies, expertise of this kind is, indeed, urgently required if the Government is to secure and preserve a conducive environment where private initiative is encouraged to lead manufacturing growth under the free and fair guidance of market forces.

Yet the implemention of a far-reaching programme of industrial restructuring entails in transition economies the mobilization and management of a massive inflow of resources, particularly in the form of private capital. Thus, Chapter 6 finally brings the reflection to an end with an overview of foreign direct investment and technology transfers in industrializing countries. Different instruments are in practice available; they are to some extent industry specific, but they can also be effectively managed by appropriate government policies aimed at maximizing their benefits for the host country.

Part II presents in some detail the design of an industrialization strategy for the Red River Delta region of Viet Nam. The Delta stretches over densely populated lowlands that comprise both the capital Hanoi and the country's largest port, Haiphong. It counts nearly a fifth of the country's population, and contributes a similar share to its total output. Yet the further growth of agricultural yields appears limited by the very density of the population in this area, and this prompted the Government to investigate the potential for manufacturing development.

Chapters 7 and 8 set the stage with background information, an overview of the prevailing policy environment as well as the institutional and regulatory framework. The pace of reform has been extremely fast under the thrust of the economic liberalization programme launched in 1986. Milestones along the way have been the waiver of the international embargo, the resumption of major bilateral and multilateral official development aid, and significant inflows of private capital. These external developments clearly exert a most beneficial effect on domestic growth prospects; they were made possible by profound reforms of economic management.

The resource base and current manufacturing industries in the Red River Delta are then reviewed in Chapter 9. Capacities already exist in the region, particularly in the form of large State-owned enterprises in such heavy industries as cement, chemicals and steel. However, the form of industrial organization is gradually evolving, as public enterprises loosen their ties with the central authority and a fast-growing class of private entrepreneurs moves into small-scale businesses.

The economic liberalization programme creates opportunites for a fuller exploitation of the region's assets. While it is relatively easy to delineate acquired advantages, it is a far more complex task to ponder the odds of resolute forays into new manufacturing ventures. Chapter 10 suggests, however, a market-friendly alternative to identify promising industries, where selective policy efforts can indeed contribute to the creation of dynamic comparative advantages.

Chapter 11 in turn translates broad strategic options into their actual implementation requirements. Governments have at their disposal an array of policy instruments to intervene; some trigger a nearly immediate supply response, while others need a longer period of time before generating their full effects. A comprehensive combination of policy moves is therefore warranted for a dynamic management of the industrialization process. The chapter concludes with practical measures to develop technological capabilities in high-growth industries while mitigating the adverse effects of a possibly uneven development pattern.

A few concluding remarks are ultimately proposed in Chapter 12. While regional authorities can be expected to hold a more accurate view on the local needs and therefore allocate public resources in a more efficient manner, the natural answer should hint at administrative decentralization, including with respect to the tax-raising capacity, of the State apparatus. Special concessions granted by the Centre to particular regions – for instance to level out possible economic disparities – inevitably entail an element of second best, and warrant a careful assessment of their costs against their expected benefits. Finally, ad hoc policy measures applied to specific regions amount to a restriction of the economic space, and equally call for a critical analysis, particularly at a time of increased integration of economic activities in a supra-national, and ultimately the global stage.

Part I

General Issues on Economic Reforms
and Industrial Restructuring
in Transition Countries

1. Long-term Perspectives on Economic Reform and Industrial Restructuring

*G. Chris Rodrigo**

Introduction: Objectives of Economic Reform and Preconditions

The primary objective of economic reform is to generate conditions for faster economic growth in the longer term. Economic growth itself is not the only or ultimate objective of countries undertaking economic reform, but it is a necessary condition for all other developmental objectives. In other words, countries that have failed to generate reasonably rapid real growth per capita over the long run have inevitably suffered a general deterioration of social and political stability. Examples that come readily to mind are Egypt, Peru, Sri Lanka and, more recently, Algeria.

However, economic growth by itself is hardly sufficient to ensure social and political stability. The revolution in the Islamic Republic of Iran took place despite substantial growth. Currently, very fast growth in China is creating serious problems of macroeconomic instability and social disorder. The complex interaction between economic and political events cannot be examined in detail in this paper, but due cognizance must be taken of this important connection.

It is also clear that no economic programme *per se* can take hold until a certain level of social and political consensus is realized at the initial stage. In the eastern Asian countries this consensus was achieved largely through the political power of authoritarian regimes. If growth is sustained, the consensus, whether implicit or explicit, is generally

*Cornell University, Ithaca, NY and National University of Singapore.

strengthened. But if growth falters political stability is undermined. In the contemporary world it is almost universally true that the legitimacy of a Government is founded on its ability to maintain rising living standards for a large portion of its population.

If the above premise is accepted, then the question arises about the extent of growth performance that is necessary to ensure social and political stability. It is clearly not enough merely to sustain positive growth. Most developing countries have achieved that already; many have also reached growth rates matching those of the developed countries. But this is not enough, since that would only maintain the existing wide disparity in consumption levels.

We live in a world caught in the throes of the information revolution. Through the mass media, people in poorer countries are increasingly aware of consumption levels and standards of living prevalent in industrial societies. This awareness is substantially enhanced by the ostentatious lifestyles of privileged social strata in their own countries. For social stability, it is necessary to achieve some degree of catch-up with these consumption levels, which necessarily entails growth rates of income per capita much higher than those commonly recorded in developed and developing countries since the Second World War.

Figure 1.1 shows a highly stylized representation of the catch-up phenomenon. The upper and lower growth trajectories represent the growth patterns of a typical industrial economy and a typical developing economy plotted against time. They both have the same growth rate of income per capita, which is what makes their growth paths linear on a log scale. The logistic-type 'S' curve is the growth path for a country that achieves catch-up in a finite period of time to all intents and purposes. An essential part of the catch-up phenomenon is that the growth rate accelerates initially to a high level. This level is maintained for a substantial period of time (say, two to three decades) before growth begins to taper off to levels normal for developed countries.

The next question is obviously whether such an optimistic scenario is even remotely feasible. Figure 1.2 depicts the actual performance of Japan and the East Asian newly industrialized countries (EA-NICs). Their growth patterns are framed within the growth patterns of India and the United States of America. Again, real GDP per capita is plotted on a log scale against time for the post war period.[1] It is clear that Japan has substantially caught up, though it started from a rather low level. The EA-NICs start from levels much closer to that of India, but have quite substantially narrowed their gap with Japan and the United States. If trends continue along the same lines, it is clear that they will eventually catch up. Hong Kong has already caught up with Japan in real terms and Singapore is close behind.

Figure 1.1   Economic growth in historical perspective:
idealized catch-up by developing countries

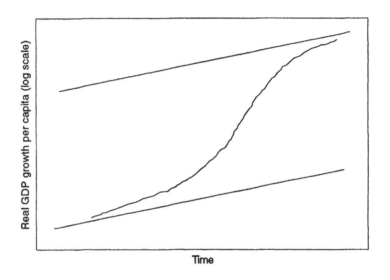

The pattern for the next tier of South-East Asian newly industrialized countries (SEA-NICs) is shown in Figure 1.3. Their performance is good but much less spectacular than that of the EA-NICs; there is no clear convergence pattern with Japan and the United States. It is clearly too early to make any definite predictions about catching up for this group of countries.

Thus, cross-country evidence shows that catching up is definitely possible. This is true not only for city-States like Singapore, but also for larger countries like the Republic of Korea, and, of course, Japan. A further conclusion is that the second tier SEA-NICs seem unable to quite match the growth rates of the EA-NICs. Hence it is necessary to consider the East Asian experience critically to determine which ingredients promote growth and which hold it back.

Figure 1.2   Growth pattern of the East Asian NICs compared to that of the United States, Japan and India

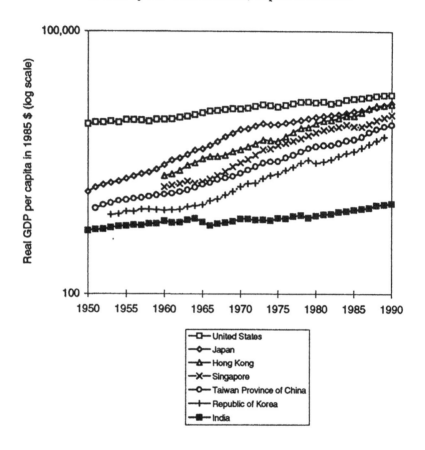

The effect of initial resource endowments is one that immediately springs to mind. Previously it was thought that valuable natural resources would confer a great advantage in the race for development. Yet the most successful economies in East Asia, Japan and the EA-NICs hardly have any resources in sizeable quantities. Some economists now argue that this shortage has compelled countries to develop the most important resource of all, the skills of their people. In the long run this has proven to be the best development strategy. It is certainly true that in these countries, educational levels and technological competence are at the highest levels reached in developing countries. The argument is expanded much further in this chapter and forms its main unifying theme.

Figure 1.3   *Growth pattern of the South-East Asian NICs compared to that of the United States, Japan and China*

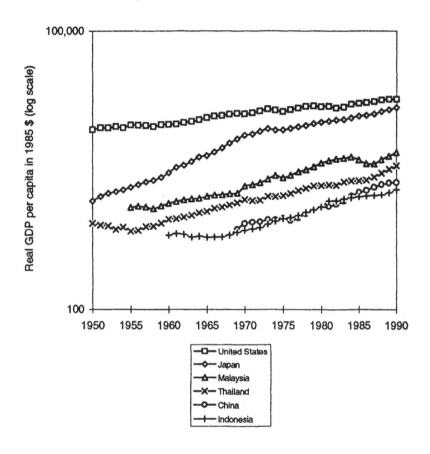

The observed features of the second tier of NICs are consistent with this initial hypothesis. Indonesia, Malaysia and Thailand are abundantly endowed with natural resources which, to a large extent, shaped their manufacturing and exports patterns. However, the level of skill and technology required for manufacturing these products is also relatively low. As indicated above, the performance of these resource-rich countries is well below that of the resource-poor EA-NICs. The overall skill-competence levels of the industrial workforce, managerial cadres and State bureaucracy in the SEA-NIC countries is also much less developed than in the first tier NICs.

Indonesia, in particular, was heavily dependent on petroleum exports and encountered serious macroeconomic adjustment problems as a consequence of the sharp decline of oil prices in the 1980s. After the shock of 1982–1983, Indonesia undertook a programme of economic reform and liberalization on its own volition. This was relatively successful and since the late 1980s, the economy has expanded rapidly, with manufactures constituting a larger part of exports than oil and other raw materials.[2] There does not appear to be any *a priori* reason why what was possible for Indonesia could not be achieved by other resource-rich nations as well.

What is the Real Wealth of Nations?

The concept of the 'wealth of nations' is one that has existed almost from the beginning of civilization. Very broadly it has been used – and is used here as well – to denote the general level of prosperity of a nation or the determinants of that prosperity. The concept of wealth, however, has been evolving over time, depending on our understanding of economics. At one time wealth was conceived of as gold, silver and precious stones, impressive buildings and monuments and anything else that cost a great deal to construct. Currently, the World Bank and other international organizations use the real GNP per capita (corrected for purchasing power parity) as the best single measure of national prosperity, at least for the purpose of international comparisons. This is also an approximate measure of the growth of overall labour productivity in the nation.

The above measure of average real income per capita arguably fails to reflect domestic work, environmental degradation and so on. All that is well known. But there are other problems that substantially detract from its use as a yardstick of economic well being. Consider, for example, the data presented in Table 1.1.

At first glance, Kuwait appears better off than Singapore while Spain is considerably ahead of the Republic of Korea. But the Republic of Korea and Singapore are strong industrial economies whose economic positions in world markets are secure to a high degree. Kuwait's wealth depends on petroleum, an exhaustible resource – which is also prone to price erosion as a commodity – and on its investment income. Spain's prosperity currently depends a great deal on agricultural exports which are very sensitive to movements in international markets.

Spain is however industrializing quickly and is becoming less dependent on price-volatile primary commodities.

Table 1.1   An inter-country comparison of real income

Country	Population (millions)	GNP/capita in US$ (1991)
Kuwait	2.0	16,150
Republic of Korea	42.4	4,400
Singapore	2.7	10,450
Spain	38.8	9,330

Source: World Development Report 1992 (World Bank).

The main point is that the wealth of the Republic of Korea and Singapore resides in the skill and industry of their people. It is therefore robust against long-term changes in technology and the economic value of particular commodities such as oil. Kuwait is vulnerable in this respect. Further, its social infrastructure is heavily dependent on foreign workers. The point is further clarified by the example of Germany after the Second World War. Even though the country was totally devastated, within a few years its industry was back to impressively high productivity levels. Unlike its physical infrastructure, the skills residing in its workforce and the efficiency of its social organization and institutions were not much affected by the devastation of war.[3]

To complete the argument, the issue can be summarized as follows. The potential real income per capita of a country depends on the productivity of its labour. Potential labour productivity in turn depends on the level of accumulation of human and physical capital in that country. Human capital represents the skill levels of its entire workforce, including managers, administrators and suppliers of various other services. Human capital depends on educational levels, but even more crucially on skills acquired through actual work experience, whether in production, administration or whatever other capacity. Physical capital is, of course, a measure of the technological leverage embodied in machines and other productivity-enhancing equipment.

Human capital is usually understood as associated with individual workers or managers. But in the modern context, people do not work in isolation. They work in small or large organizations and in business or economic environments that substantially contribute to overall productivity. The productivity of a given worker in a multinational company such as IBM is significantly greater than that of the same worker operating in a newly set up computer company elsewhere; the operating procedures in IBM are likely to be highly developed and efficient, compared to that of a start-up company, and business transactions also take place more efficiently in an environment in which business institutions are more highly developed.

It is clear that the level of development of business organizations and economic institutions contribute substantially to the level of overall productivity. The same argument can be extended to the efficiency or competence of the State administrative structure. Business activity is monitored and regulated by a host of State organizations which collect taxes, control imports and exports, issue licences of various sorts, arbitrate disputes, mediate in industrial conflicts or provide primary security. Some State bodies engage directly in vital economic activities such as the provision of power and transport.

If the efficiency of the State administrative structures is added to the degree of development of economic institutions and business organizations, the accumulation of this composite economic capability could plausibly be labelled as 'social-infrastructural capital'. The prefix 'social' serves a dual purpose here. First, it serves to distinguish the concept from physical infrastructural capital which also contributes to overall economic productivity in well-understood ways. Second, it helps distinguish the social aspect of economic capability from 'human capital' which at the present time is associated with the individual accumulation of education and skills. A broader and perhaps more consistent interpretation of human capital ought to include the social-infrastructural component along with the individual components.

The overall productivity of economic effort at the level of the nation-State then depends on four interrelated, but distinct, accumulations of capital. These are human capital, physical capital, social-infrastructural capital and physical-infrastructural capital. Here, capital is used in the general sense of any accumulation that enhances the productivity of human labour. Taken together, these accumulations constitute the economic capability of a nation (ECN),[4] which is ultimately the decisive measure of its wealth. The fastest path to building up ECN is the principal objective of economic reform.

Sources of Productivity Growth in East and South-East Asia

It is interesting to examine the performance of Japan, East Asia and South-East Asia in the light of the above discussion of the basic determinants of productivity growth. The overall effect of the accumulation of economic capability or ECN at the national level is represented by the growth of overall labour productivity. In growth accounting studies, it is customary to separate the growth of labour productivity into two components:

contribution of physical capital per worker

labour productivity growth =   +

contribution of economic efficiency growth

In Table 1.2 labour productivity growth is approximated by the average annual growth of GDP per capita. The second column represents the contribution to growth of direct capital investment per worker. The difference between these two is the contribution of economic efficiency growth; it represents the portion of ECN growth that is not directly attributable to the expansion of physical capital per worker. This differential or 'residual' growth component, called total factor productivity (TFP), is given in the third column of the table.

It is immediately clear that the contribution of TFP growth is substantial for Japan and the East Asian NICs as a whole. It is significantly less so for the South-East Asian nations listed here. GDP growth per capita is also less for this group. Singapore alone is something of an anomaly: its GDP per capita growth places it squarely within the East Asian rank; but its TFP growth is more akin to that of the South-East Asian group. Its high growth seemingly derives from an extraordinarily high rate of capital investment sustained over nearly three decades.[5]

Table 1.2   Sources of growth in Asian newly industrialized
              countries or areas
              (average over 1960–1989)

Country	GDP growth per capita (%)	Growth from investment (%)	Residual TFP growth (%)
China (Taiwan Province)	7.0	3.5	3.5
Hong Kong	5.8	2.3	3.5
Indonesia	3.2	2.0	1.2
Japan	5.5	2.0	3.5
Malaysia	4.0	2.9	1.1
Republic of Korea	6.6	3.4	3.2
Singapore	6.2	4.9	1.3
Thailand	4.6	2.2	2.4

Source: The East Asian Miracle, World Bank (1993).

Leaving aside the case of Singapore, the above table shows that the direct contribution of physical capital to overall productivity growth is roughly similar for the entire group, Japan, the EA-NICs and the SEA-NICs. This direct component ranges from 2 per cent to about 3.5 per cent per annum with Taiwan Province of China, and the Republic of Korea closer to the upper bound and most of the others closer to the lower figure.

But the overall growth of GDP per capita is significantly higher for the EA-NICs and Japan than for the three SEA-NICs. For the most part, this marked difference in performance is the result of the extra bonus gained from the TFP residual, which ranges from 3.2 to 3.5 per cent per annum in China (Taiwan Province), Japan, Hong Kong and Republic of Korea, sustained over a period of nearly three decades. This is a truly extraordinary achievement;[6] it accounts for the difference between growth that is merely high as in the case of Indonesia, Malaysia and Thailand and growth that is exceptional as in China (Taiwan Province), Hong Kong and the Republic of Korea. Sustained over a period of two or three decades, this differential adds up to a very large gap indeed.

The comparison made above is between the EA-NICs and the SEA-NICs which themselves have achieved growth rates of per capita income that are well above the norm for developing countries. This point has already been discussed in the introductory section. There it was established that, taken in the context of the performance of developing countries as a whole, the EA-NIC rates of growth enable catching up with the advanced countries, but that even the high growth of the SEA-NICs makes this possibility uncertain for the foreseeable future. It should be noted that a 7 per cent growth rate of per capita income enables a doubling of real living standards in 10 years, while at a reduced 4 per cent per annum, it takes 18 years to record the same progress. The productivity bonus can significantly shorten the time taken to achieve particular development targets. Furthermore, high growth often leads to high saving rates, as consumption grows more slowly than income.

The conventional wisdom is that high growth requires high levels of investment sustained over long periods of time. The East Asian NICs have certainly managed that with extraordinarily high levels of savings and investment. But the main point developed in this paper is that the critical difference lies in tapping the potential productivity bonus illustrated in Table 1.2. As discussed above, physical investment accounts only for the relatively modest gains shown in column 2. This is the direct effect of investment, accessible with relative ease by most countries that have relatively stable internal conditions.[7] The crucial difference lies in using direct physical investment to leverage the potential productivity bonus shown in column 3; that indeed is the important lesson to be learned from the East Asian experience.

Where does this productivity bonus come from? In the previous section it was shown that long-run overall labour productivity growth in a nation is determined by the following four variants of capital accumulations:

Physical capital	Physical infrastructural capital
Human capital	Social infrastructural capital

They are all appropriately described as capital because they can be accumulated and have the principal effect of raising labour productivity. They also all exhibit the property of depreciating over time along with technological change. The first two largely determine the gains shown in column 2 of Table 1.2 and the last, or bottom, pair is responsible for the TFP bonus. The physical accumulations are of course well understood by most people interested in economic development. Human capital is still, somewhat regrettably, associated with initial education levels and health and living standards. It is argued above that there is much more to it; the main component of human capital should be the level of skill accumulation acquired by experience, to which formal education is only a favourable or enabling condition. Social infrastructural capital includes the levels of organizational and institutional development in society and the skill and efficiency of the State administrative authorities.

How can High Productivity Growth be Achieved?

Despite the differences of outlook that continue to prevail among economists, there is now a remarkable degree of agreement on the main features of successful economic reform. For example, most economists and policy makers tend to agree that the private sector should be the principal engine of growth. In other words, market forces must be encouraged and given considerable freedom to operate. There continues to be differences about the degree to which economic activity should be controlled and about the timing and sequencing of reforms. But the emphasis everywhere is on promoting business-friendly institutions, both formal ones such as financial institutions and informal ones such as codes of behaviour.

The task here is to provide an explanation of how market-oriented economic reform translates into higher productivity growth. In terms of the conceptual framework developed above, productivity growth depends on ECN which in turn hinges on the four capital accumulations described above. The specifics of productivity-enhancing ECN are more commonly referred to by the term 'technological capability'.[8] The desirable outcome of economic reform that constitute the main elements of ECN are briefly described in Appendix 1, along with some theoretical and conceptual issues. The emphasis here is to highlight the empirically established insights on how and why market-friendly institutions lead to faster growth of productivity.

The role of physical capital and physical infrastructure in productivity growth is widely understood and does not bear elaboration. The continual replacement of machines by better machines embodying more advanced technologies is a central feature of contemporary culture, and so is the steady expansion of physical structures devoted to transport, communications, health, education and other infrastructural services. The contribution of enormously high investment in machines and physical structures to productivity is palpably the defining feature of modern industrial society.

The role of human capital and social infrastructural capital is less well understood. New developments in the way we think about economic growth have brought the importance of human capital to the forefront, as an important contributor to productivity growth. But it is still mostly associated with education and not so much with work-acquired skill. The importance of good organization and management is also recognized, as is the value of market-friendly institutions. But economic analysis does not at present include these accumulations of social infrastructural capital along with narrowly defined human capital in the determination of productivity. Good institutions and organizations are also, of course, a generalized form of human capital, but this extension of meaning is not adopted here to conform with current usage in the economic literature.

The principal argument advanced in this paper is then the following. Market-oriented reforms lead to sharper competition and faster learning in carrying out economically significant tasks. This learning is accumulated as human capital and social infrastructural capital. The former is accumulated in the individual worker and the latter is incorporated in the organizational forms and administrative structures, as explained above. These accumulations raise the propensity of individuals and organizations to work more efficiently, which is of course the essence of productivity growth. The concrete ways in which these processes operate is described in the next two sections which draw on a number of empirical studies. The argument is then generalized and brought to a conclusion in the last section.

Productivity Growth in Industrial Organizations

The arguments of the above section can be illustrated by considering some concrete empirical results on how productivity growth takes place in industrial organizations. Pack (1987) has shown that productivity growth, at the level of the firm, is the consequence of three types of efficiency gains:

Gains in technical efficiency
Improvements in allocative efficiency
Long-term technological change

The role of technological change is of course well understood. Conventional economic analysis has focused mostly on the issue of allocative efficiency and neglected technical efficiency.[9] Recently, following detailed estimates of productive efficiency carried out at firm and plant levels, the emphasis has shifted to technical inefficiency and the mechanisms by which these are overcome to enhance growth. Pack notes that 'economists and industrial engineers had devoted relatively little effort to either measuring or understanding the sources of low productivity in manufacturing in developing countries'. Today technical efficiency is known to be quantitatively far more important than allocative efficiency. There is also a growing body of literature on its identification and statistical estimation.[10]

Technical efficiency is defined with respect to the best practice production frontier. This is illustrated in Figure 1.4 which plots the distribution of productive efficiency for individual firms in a particular industry in a single country; each point represents the capital and labour inputs required for unit output. The lower envelope of the distribution is the domestic best practice frontier (DBPF) which covers a range of technologies with varying capital/labour ratios. The theoretical optimum production point is *A*, where the factor price line *BC* touches the DBPF. If some parametric form is assumed for the technical efficiency distribution, the DBPF can be derived by a statistical method which is briefly discussed later in this section.

Figure 1.5 shows the productive efficiency of a single firm operating at point *P*. The minimum cost point is *A* and not *R*, for a given factor price line *BC* and production DBPF. The Farrel measure of technical inefficiency is *PR/OR*. The price inefficiency *RS/OS* is a measure of allocative inefficiency arising from excessive use of capital. The DBPF would in general lie above the international best practice frontier (IBPF). The concept of technological inefficiency does not arise (except perhaps in education and in the health care industry) since technology differentials across countries are considered acceptable and even desirable by most economists, at least for the historical short term.

Figure 1.4   Variation of plant level productive efficiency within the same industry in a single developing country with negligible competition

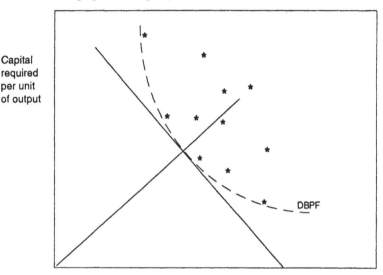

Labour required per unit of output

Source: Adapted from Pack, 1988.
DBPF = domestic best practice frontier

With regard to éstimates of technical efficiency in developing countries, Pack's pioneering work is the most important. Pack began with plant-level studies of manufacturing industry in developing countries such as Kenya and the Philippines. He discusses how and why particular technology choices are made and the numerous ways in which inefficiency (with respect to the DBPF) are generated. Pack further states that most developing countries operate well below the IBPF. Productivity advance through technical efficiency gain is realized when these inefficiencies are deliberately corrected by better industrial engineering techniques, typically under the pressure of competition. Competitive pressures induce firms to move towards the DBPF as shown in Figure 1.6, thereby raising aggregate productivity in that sector.

Figure 1.5   Potential productivity gains for a single plant from technical and allocative advances and technological change

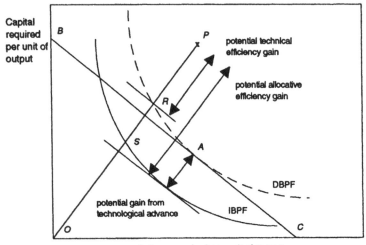

Labour required per unit of output

Source: Adapted from Pack, 1988.
DBPF = domestic best practice frontier
IBPF = international best practice frontier

Pack found that technical efficiency within the same industry using the same technology varied widely.[11] He figures that, on an aggregate basis, the movement to best practice (i.e., elimination of technical inefficiency) would add 25–40 per cent to overall output in Egypt, Ghana and India, whereas improved allocative efficiency would enhance output by 7–17 per cent. Caves and Barton (1990) quote previous studies of technical efficiency estimates for various countries: 55 per cent for Colombian apparel and footwear industries, 62.5 per cent for Brazilian manufacturing industries, 62–68 per cent for Indonesia's weaving industry and 71–94 per cent for an aggregate of 10 French manufacturing industries.

In the industrial economy, productivity growth derives from the three effects shown in Figure 1.5: rising technical efficiency as firms move towards the DBPF through learning, gains in allocative efficiency as firms make new investment decisions more consistent with market signals, technological advance derived from new – usually imported – equipment as firms move towards the IBPF. Gains from technical efficiency dominate allocative efficiency gains as many firms in developing regions operate well below their DBPF.

Figure 1.6   Variability of plant level productive efficiency within the same industry in a single country with competition

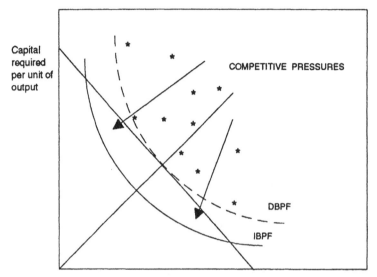

Labour required per unit of output

DBPF = domestic best practice frontier
IBPF = international best practice frontier

Productivity gains obtained through progress in technical efficiency is achieved by conscious and deliberate efforts that overcome inefficiencies in the production process. This raising of efficiency constitutes industrial learning at different levels and of different types. Learning by doing is an area on which there is considerable discussion in economic literature. The issue is widely discussed in the business literature as well, since many modern industries exhibit a learning curve; average variable (production) costs decline with cumulative output as workers, supervisors and managers build up skills around a specific production process. The skill accumulation process works not only in direct production activities such as fabrication, machining and assembly, but also in support activities such as inventory control of inputs and finished goods, scheduling and production planning. A more detailed account of industrial learning processes is given in Appendix 2.

In practice, technical efficiency growth is dependent on the technology used and can be boosted by technological innovation. A very important characteristic of industrial learning processes is highlighted by Young (1991) in his model of bounded learning by doing. He begins with two empirical observations: the first is that innovations exhibit considerable spillover across firms and industries; the second is that beyond a certain threshold, learning curves plateau out so that productivity advance through learning is essentially bounded.

Young argues that:

> learning by doing can be conceived of as the exploration and actualization of the productive potential of new technologies, if you will, a series of minor technical innovations that are learned from a major technical breakthrough. Thus the development of new productive technologies . . . initially leads to rapid learning by doing. After some time, however, the productive capability of these new technologies is exhausted, and learning by doing slows and perhaps ultimately stops. In the absence of the introduction of new technical processes, it is likely that learning by doing cannot be sustained.

Young develops a model of growth based on learning by doing with spillovers across goods. Trade also plays a role in the model by accelerating technical progress and growth under certain conditions. The model clearly embodies many of the empirical features of the growth process.

What is of principal interest here is the conceptualization of bounded learning by doing. This is adapted somewhat from Young and represented here by the diagram of Figure 1.7. Here, learning by doing proceeds, unevenly, along a particular technology represented by the Technology 1 curve. At some point there is a shift to a superior technology with a greater potential for productivity gain and the learning-by-doing process continues along the Technology 2 curve. At the initial transition point, the operational productivity may very well drop below the previous value, though not always. But the transition is made because of the expectation of longer term gains.

Some important issues are raised here. In countries where markets are characterized by sharp competition, technology transitions occur well ahead of the productivity plateau, as firms strive to gain a competitive edge over each other. With shorter technology cycle times the pace of innovation and, more importantly for this study, the associated rate of learning and productivity growth is higher. It is important to emphasize that competition accelerates two related productivity enhancing processes: the first is faster technological change; the second is the rate of advance of technical efficiency, which is faster in the initial parts of the learning curve, for all technologies.

Figure 1.7   Bounded learning by doing: technological change and productivity growth

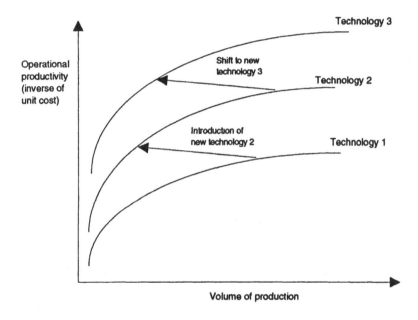

Similar arguments are advanced by Lall[12] who analyses the acquisition of firm-level technological capability (FTC). Lall distinguishes three aspects of FTC, following the technology literature: 'technological mastery' refers to the skills and competence needed to operate an installed technology efficiently; 'minor innovations' describe adaptations and improvements that raise productivity of installed technology; 'major innovation' refers to the introduction of entirely new products and processes, usually through new capital investment. Clearly all three types of capability are necessary for a firm to maintain viability in a dynamic competitive environment. The concept of technical efficiency

advance earlier described is approximately equivalent to gains resulting from minor innovations.

Technological progress involves improvement in all three of the
above areas and leads to productivity gains. There is considerable
learning necessary in all areas. Lall shows that every major innovation
is subject to innumerable minor innovations after introduction. Minor
innovations are represented by the jagged upward movement of productivity along a single technology curve in Figure 1.7. This, together
with the migration to the best practice frontier, are the sources of on-
going productivity growth, and reflect the degree of dynamism of the
firm. The introduction of an altogether new major innovation is represented in Figure 1.7 as a one-time shift from one technology curve to
the next. Major innovation may initially lower productivity but eventually leads to substantial gains over the displaced technology.

One of the central arguments made in this chapter is that learning
and productivity growth are dual aspects of a single phenomenon. This
yields a new perspective on economic growth: i.e., growth is fastest in
periods of rapid technological change because of the enhanced learning
potential at that time. Furthermore, competitive struggle between firms
is essential for sustaining the momentum of the growth process
through the drive for productivity advantage. Young argues that in the
pre-modern era, even intense economic activity did not lead to sustained economic growth because of the slow pace of technical change
that generated little scope for learning activity.

How Institutions and Human Capital Contribute to ECN

Firms are, of course, the most palpable entities on the economic land-
scape. The way learning and productivity growth in firms contribute to
ECN is easy to understand. But learning and productivity growth take
place in the course of institutional evolution as well. In every country
economic transactions take place within a network of institutions that
are set up in historical time. North[13] defines institutions as 'rules,
enforcement characteristics of rules, and norms of behaviour that
structure repeated human interaction'. When particular sets of economic
transactions are frequently repeated because they benefit all participants, the pattern of transaction crystallizes into an institution, much as
a sustained flow of water will cut its own channel in the ground,
thereby facilitating subsequent passage.

Institutions come into being through natural economic evolution or are deliberately set up. Their positive economic role is to markedly reduce the uncertainty associated with new economic activity and reduce transaction costs. Institutions can also play a negative role when they become dysfunctional through economic evolution. They are difficult to replace because of entrenched inertia in human agents and social groups. The setting up of efficient business institutions, however, is enormously pertinent to the issue of national economic capability; indeed healthy institutions are difficult to set up and involve considerable social investment or social learning.

Institutional development does not have to follow the same path in all countries. Lall notes that institutional innovation or adaptation can serve to bypass inefficient markets or restore their proper functioning.[14] In fact pre-capitalist institutions, such as the Chinese clan networks, have been very effectively pressed into service to make up for the absence of modern financial institutions in East Asia. Thus, institutions can even substitute for government intervention in correcting imperfect markets.

Institutions are vital to the functioning of the entire business sector. They facilitate economic transactions and substitute for absent or undeveloped markets. There are formal and informal institutions all of which grow and develop along with successful economic activity. Formal institutions include business and professional associations, training centres, technical colleges and universities, standards institutes, legal bodies, financial institutions, and so on. Informal institutions cover established business practices and codes of behaviour, networks of business contacts and, indeed, a host of inherited nation-specific business-cultural norms.

The other major determinant of ECN is human capital in all its forms. Numerous research studies show that education, training and other forms of skill formation are critically important to industrial competence and productivity. Basic literacy and numeracy are essential for the entire workforce in all modern industry. Vocational and technical training are necessary for technical personnel and for skilled workers in more advanced industries. The complexity of technical training rises with the level of technical sophistication of the production processes.

In addition to technical training, on-the-job training is needed for supervisors and junior managers and often supplemented by more formal management training in-house or in external institutions. Lall touches only superficially on the issue of managerial skills and training, which he sees merely as a part of 'technical' skill. It is clear that a range of educational institutions, from technical and vocational schools to engineering departments and management schools in universities, are necessary to supply the demand for formal education. Managerial and business skills, even more than technical skills, are the scarcest productive resource in many developing countries.[15] As the technologies employed reach present frontiers, such as in the Republic of Korea and Taiwan Province of China, pure science capability also becomes important.

Lall makes a number of points in relation to the supply and demand for the above skills. First, as technologies change rapidly, intensive in-firm training becomes necessary to create new skills on a continuous basis. Second, for the efficient diffusion of skills through the industrial structure by migration of personnel, these skills need to be sharply demarcated, recognized and, not least, certified accurately. Third, the quality of technical education is as important as its quantity, and fourth, the distribution of technical skills supplied must match the specific requirements of the industrial economy.

This last point applies more generally to all productive resources: 'It is the productive deployment of capabilities that we are concerned with, not the potential existing in, say, stocks of under-utilized capital, engineering manpower or academic knowledge'.[16] Despite common assumptions to the contrary, there is a high degree of complementarity between skills and physical resources; thus, investment in education can be wasted if it is not geared to the evolution of industry. For this reason, wastage associated with superfluous resources are much less likely in market-driven systems where investment in resources is guided by expected returns. The problem is, in fact, the reverse: there is insufficient investment in human resource development because the returns cannot be completely appropriated by the firm. Consequently, public investment has to play a large role in the development of human capital.

From the analysis developed in the previous section, it is clear that skills, competence and firm-level training acquired through production and other economic activity constitute a very important part of the total human capital that bears directly on productive efficiency. Formal education is actually more in the nature of an enabling condition for the accumulation of experience capital. With regard to human capital Lall states:

> A large part of this is measurable, but some is not: the experience and firm training component is almost impossible to measure in a comparable way, as is the quality of formal education. In addition, human capital is conditioned by the sociocultural legacy and past experience of commerce and industry – again these are difficult to measure precisely and have to be ignored.

Conclusion: Building Economic Capability

The two previous sections discuss in some detail the processes of skill accumulation within firms and in the national social matrix in which they operate. The latter include institutions, organizations and the administrative framework. It has been shown that skill accumulation of all types contributes to productivity growth and can therefore be conceptualized as the accumulation of some non-physical forms of capital. It has also been established that competitive market conditions greatly enhance the rate of learning and productivity growth. Thus the purpose of economic reform is to generate conditions that bring about faster accumulation of this non-physical capital, which has been separated here into human capital and social-infrastructural capital.

The potential gains are greater for less developed countries, but these are not automatic. They are realized only in export-oriented regimes where competitive pressures accelerate learning at all levels through technological change, new product development and quality and productivity advance (as illustrated in Figures 1.4–1.6). It is the differential responses that account for the variations across nations.

Finally, there is the practical problem of modelling human and social infrastructural capital accumulation. Such capital is not deliberately invested in and not subject to conventional cost accounting. The accumulation is contingent on various other variables and on macroeconomic conditions, such as the degree of outward orientation.

A conceptual representation of the various linkages is given in Figure 1.8. This model separates industrial activity into production for exports and for the domestic market. There are, of course, spillovers and externalities between the two sectors, represented by the arrows between them. Both types of activity lead to physical capital and non-physical capital accumulation. The latter includes the growth of market-friendly institutions and business practices within society and the competence of governing bureaucracies. Both types of capital raise productivity in symmetrical fashion. The special role of exports is shown by double arrows: exports promote faster human and social capital accumulation and faster physical capital growth by relaxing foreign exchange constraints for capital imports.

Figure 1.8   Determinants of labour productivity: the extra benefit of export-oriented manufacturing

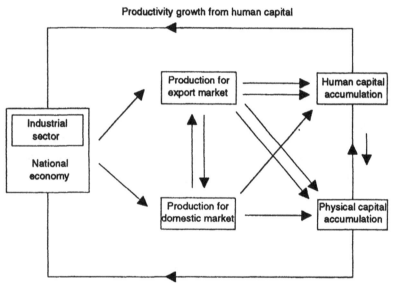

Productivity growth from human capital

Industrial sector

National economy

Production for export market

Human capital accumulation

Production for domestic market

Physical capital accumulation

Productivity growth from physical capital

The main question of interest here is the extent to which growth would be enhanced if East Asian type market conditions and disciplines were overlayed on more regular development patterns in particular countries. The essence of this process would be faster growth of export-oriented industry, inducing faster learning in all organized areas of the economy by the mechanisms described in the previous two sections.

Notes

1. The data are taken from the most recent Penn World Tables Version 5.5 (Summers and Heston, 1991), which corrects for purchasing power parity.
2. The adjustment experience of Indonesia is discussed in Thorbecke (1991).
3. See Dornbusch (1993) for a discussion of Germany's post-war economic history.
4. ECN is referred to as 'technological capability' in Lall (1990, 1992) which contain exhaustive descriptions of its different aspects. This terminology is not used here since in common parlance the word 'technological' usually has a much narrower meaning.
5. See in particular Young (1992) for an elaborate analysis of this peculiar feature.
6. See Pack (1992) for a discussion of this issue in the case of Taiwan Province of China.
7. The separation of the growth rate of output per capita into a direct component attributable to capital deepening (i.e., a higher level of capital per worker) and the total factor productivity residual depends to some extent on the assumptions made in the analysis. Thus other analysts have come up with TFP measures that are somewhat lower than the World Bank estimates. The variability of TFP measures does not, however, affect the conclusions drawn in this paper; as long as the estimation methodology is applied consistently, the relative difference between nations and groups of nations shows up with the same stark clarity. This issue is discussed in Rodrigo (1994).
8. Lall (1990, 1992), World Bank (1993).
9. Technical efficiency gain is equivalent to the overcoming of X-inefficiencies in Leibenstein's terminology.
10. See Pack (1987, 1988), Caves and Barton (1990), Caves (1992) and World Bank (1993).
11. This issue is pertinent not just for industry in developing countries; in their study of efficiency in US manufacturing industries, Caves and Barton (1990) state 'data on distributions of cost and efficiency levels within industries regularly reveal what seem to be striking amounts of technical inefficiency'. They ask why technical efficiency has received so little attention when it is so much more important than allocative efficiency in reducing costs. One important reason for this, they argue, is the inadequacy of the conventional theory; an inefficient firm or manager fails in effect to maximize profits or utility, a case poorly substantiated in the neoclassical paradigm. Caves (1992) remarks 'the hypothesis of profit maximization has mutated into an axiom ever ready to deny any allegation of productive inefficiency'. Theory, after all, is not only a framework but also a filter for the comprehension of material reality.
12. Lall (1990, 1992) analyses the range of activities and investment necessary for a developing nation to achieve rapid industrial growth. It is important to note that the term 'technological' is now used in a broader sense; it encompasses not just science-based innovations embodied in productive machinery and processes, but also technical or production engineering efficiencies, modern business institutions and so on, as will be described later. Lall uses 'technological capability' in the sense of the range of skills needed in the country as a whole to operate industry efficiently under competitive conditions. There is firm level technological capability (FTC) which refers to the characteristics of successful firms, and national technological capability (NTC) which is the broad set of national capabilities, institutions and conditions necessary for firms to operate efficiently within its matrix. FTC and NTC constitute what is called ECN in this chapter.
13. The nature and role of institutions is explored in Thorbecke (1990) and North (1989).
14. Lall (1990) quotes a long string of publications to document the scope and diversity of institutional structures analysed in developing countries.
15. This issue is discussed in detail for the case of Sri Lanka in Rodrigo (1987).
16. Lall (1990).

Appendix 1. What Economic Reform Should Bring About

In any discussion of how growth-promoting economic reform is implemented, it is useful to list briefly what specific outcomes can be expected from successful reform leading to economic growth of catch-up magnitude, again drawn from the experience of East Asia. These outcomes are not merely the consequences of rapid growth, but are also enabling conditions that promote further sustained growth. For example, it was argued that high growth would lead to a high savings rate, as consumption lagged behind income. But high savings, in turn, promote high investment levels which lead to faster growth. This statement would not make sense in an open-loop causal model in which cause and effect are rigidly separated into distinct compartments.

But economic growth, like many other natural and social processes, is not an open loop: once a strong growth impulse is initiated it creates institutions and an accumulation of industrial capability that further facilitate growth. To use terminology drawn from control theory, there is positive feedback from effect to cause that reinforces the original growth impulse.[1] To represent such processes, we need a closed-loop model in which some effects react back on the original causation, either promoting or inhibiting its operation.

Such closed-loop causation, or feedback from effect to cause is quite common in many dynamic social processes. The economics profession, in particular, is belatedly coming to realize that growth processes cannot be understood in terms of simple cause-effect logic and conventional equilibrium models. There is recognition now that in the real world externalities and feedback processes are common; increasing returns to scale are found in many industries and markets are often imperfect. Growth is a messy disequilibrium process with multiple equilibria and path dependence as unavoidable realities. The actual growth path chosen depends on expectations, which are not naively rational but limited by incomplete information and conditioned by institutions.[2]

The key point in all of the above for launching a successful growth strategy is as follows: it is crucially necessary to get right the initial orientation and the initial mix of growth-enabling conditions. Once this difficult initial stage of reform is past, a market-driven growth process will generate its own supporting social structures and institutions. Thereafter, growth becomes largely self-sustaining. However, the initial package of reforms is extraordinarily difficult to achieve and relatively few developing countries have got beyond this threshold.

Within the last decade or so, there has been a strong revival of interest in growth economics, and in particular in the role of invention, innovation and technical change in the growth process of the advanced industrial nations as well as of the NICs.[3] For this study the critical question is how technology adoption in the East Asian NICs, which is an important source of productivity growth, is related to the general development of industrial capability and human capital. This issue is examined in detail below.

At the present time, developments in new growth theory do not seem to represent much more than ad hoc modifications to the neoclassical framework. It has not led to operationally useful constructs; but the ferment generated has spawned a number of innovative approaches which are leading to a broader and deeper consideration of the sources of long-term growth. We may well be on the threshold of a Kuhnian paradigm shift in economic theory, but that is something that remains to be seen.

While formal economic theory has yet to catch up with a comprehensive explanation of long-term progress, applied economists have already delineated the broad contours of catch-up growth. The desirable outcomes presented here are consistent with the ideas, approaches and empirically established insights deriving from Lall, Pack, Amsden, Wade and others. It should be apparent by now that the perspective adopted here is somewhat at variance with official views of the World Bank and the IMF on economic reform, especially as embodied in their stabilization and structural adjustment (SSA) programmes.[4]

The main features or outcomes of successful economic reform, derived as explained above, are as follows:

- An *adequate institutional framework* that is business friendly and promotes market-based transactions is a very necessary part of economic reform. The positive economic role of institutions is to markedly reduce the uncertainty associated with new economic activity and reduce transaction costs.[5] Some of these institutions are formal and explicit, such as regulatory and financial institutions and a legal framework that supports the integrity of private property and formal contracts. The value of financial institutions, for instance, is widely accepted. Less well understood is the value of informal institutions, representing good business practices and popular acceptance or adaptation to market-based transactions. A sound and efficient institutional framework is an important outcome of a healthy growth strategy. It is also something that strongly promotes further growth, and is a prime example of an outcome that generates beneficial positive feedback, as earlier described.

- A well-functioning and relatively distortion-free *system of markets* for goods and services, capital, labour and intermediate inputs is likewise essential. The resulting system of realistic prices is absolutely necessary for reasonably efficient economic activity. Where distortions such as subsidies and tariffs are deliberately introduced in line with particular industrial policies, they must be short-lived, with termination schedules clearly marked out.

- Almost everyone agrees that a *steadily growing manufacturing sector* is a very necessary outcome of successful reform. Since the growth of domestic markets is insufficient to support the rates of growth deemed desirable, such a strategy involves the growth of exports. Manufacturing industry must be induced to become internationally competitive in the longer term, though subsidies and protection are not ruled out in the short term. An associated outcome of a dynamic industrial sector is a rapidly growing industrial labour force and a professional middle class, with rapidly improving living standards as urban wages rise in line with productivity. This is seen by many as an important force for the growth of modern, secular social institutions and political stability in general.

- The crucial benefit deriving from *exports* is associated with manufactures rather than mere commodities. Hence it is necessary for developing countries to shift the balance of exports towards manufactures away from resource-intensive products.

- The growth of real wages means that to maintain international competitiveness, the *technological basis of industry* must be periodically upgraded. This is very much in line with what has happened in East Asia and occurs normally when markets function well.

- Successful reform and rapid growth will give a strong boost to the *expansion of education* at all levels. Education must expand sufficiently to meet the industry's demand for skilled workers, managerial cadres and technically qualified personnel. Universal primary education and generalized secondary education are also considered to be very important components of any growth strategy. Again, the spread of professional education, science and technology will strengthen modern, secular cultural values and outlook.

- Strong industrial growth should lead to rapid *growth in agriculture* as well, with rising wages and productivity. Higher productivity should lead to a flow of labour towards industrial employment. Of course, this process will occur relatively smoothly only if necessary agrarian reforms are implemented, as happened in the Republic of Korea and Taiwan Province of China.

- If the above processes work well, then one would expect a *growing supply of well-paid jobs* for young people from non-urban backgrounds. This is obviously an important precondition for political stability.

- A faster and *closer integration with the world economy,* and in particular with the industrialized nations, is to be expected as a consequence of rapid trade-oriented economic growth. This is also an outcome as well as an enabling condition for rapid industrial growth, as outlined above. The social consequences are mixed since the influx of foreign cultural practices could create some tension within inherited value systems. That, however, is an inevitable part of contemporary growth and no country can insulate itself in the long term.

The final, bottom-line benefit from economic reform is all-round economic prosperity which benefits all segments of society. It is of course impossible to ensure that everybody benefits to a comparable extent from market-based reforms. But if the rise in living standards is substantial for most sections of the society, as has been observed in the economies of China (Taiwan Province), Hong Kong, Republic of Korea and Singapore, then serious political dissension usually tapers off and social stability tends to prevail. Precisely because inequality in living standards will continue to persist for the foreseeable future in all countries, it is vitally necessary that overall growth rates are high enough so that substantial improvement eventually trickles down to the most disadvantaged groups.

It should be re-emphasized that the reforms needed to bring about these outcomes must be jointly implemented as a comprehensive package, since they are mutually necessary to generate self-sustaining growth. In other words, if crucial components are missing or inadequately implemented, the overall benefit may fall well below expectations and thus undermine the credibility of the reforms and the necessary public support.

Notes

1. The existence of such two-way causality in economics, and indeed in all social science, has been described by many analysts (Sah and Stiglitz 1989, Stiglitz 1991, 1992, Arthur 1990). Such positive feedback loops are described as 'virtuous circles' or 'vicious circles' in the classical economic literature.
2. The case is put forcefully by Stiglitz (1991), Nelson (1990) and Krugman (1990, 1991, 1992) and more mildly by many other leading economists including Arrow (1991). Dornbusch (1990) excoriates the IMF model of structural adjustment, where the important questions at issue are solved by resort to assumptions, which manifestly do not hold in practice. While such subversive ideas have been often heard at the periphery of the empire, the present period is characterized by dissentient voices raised within Rome itself. Krugman, in particular, speculates that economic theory was driven by an endogenous logic along the path of least mathematical resistance. He argues that formal theory is now acquiring sophistication and flexibility to handle the difficult issues of real-world economics which were raised in ad hoc fashion by early development theorists and then abandoned in the drive for rigour.
3. Rosenberg (1982), Dosi et al. (1988), Lundvall (1992) and Nelson (1993).
4. The generalizations presented in the World Bank's recent *East Asian Miracle* (1993) are also somewhat close to this emerging consensus, but they do not by any means represent official Bank policy at the present time.
5. See North (1989) and Lall (1990).

Appendix 2.   Skill Accumulation Through Learning in Industry[1]

Potential for skill accumulation by learning in industrial activity is different for different activities. Important insights into the critical economic significance of learning effects have been developed by Amsden in the East Asian context. She argues that learning effects are greatest in skill-intensive industries, less so in capital-intensive industries and least in unskilled labour-intensive assembly operations. Skills are built up through a combination of formal education (though not always) and on-the-job experience. She describes also skill accumulation in political leadership and bureaucracy, in short in the entire social infrastructure.

A detailed account of learning dynamics and efficiency gains in different component activities in the spinning and weaving industries is given by Pack. He shows that often task-level efficiency in Kenya and the Philippines can be high in comparison with the textile industry practice in the United Kingdom of Great Britain and Northern Ireland. But overall efficiency is low because higher, more aggregate activity is performed at lower levels of efficiency. The critical weakness is often in the area of production management. The crucial lesson here is that even relatively unskilled workers in developing countries can reach international norms of task efficiency rapidly through learning by doing, but management skills are much less amenable to informal learning; these have to be painstakingly acquired by some combination of formal vocational training and on-the-job apprenticeship with experienced managers.

This is an important issue since it highlights a blind spot in the conventional theory that sees East Asian export success as depending on the selection of industries intensive in unskilled labour, in accordance with allocative efficiency considerations. Pack, Amsden and others have argued that the skills of foremen and supervisors played an important role even in labour-intensive processes in East Asia. These critical managerial skills in turn were inherited from the period of Japanese occupation.

The importance of production skill accumulation in a nation's economic progress is cogently described by Amsden. She argues that it is a delusion to think that these can be purchased simply because one operates in a market economy; these skills have to be acquired in the course of production and, unlike physical capital, cannot be imported:

> such skills and knowledge are necessary to import foreign technology success-fully, to produce more efficiently, or to graduate to production processes re-quiring still more skill and knowledge. They complement but *cannot be re-placed* by skill and knowledge acquired off the job, in research and training institutes, or via imports. They arise largely because technology can never be entirely explicit or codifiable, which is what neo-classical theory assumes when it takes technology to be universally available in blueprints.

She further argues that 'because technology is more tacit the more skill intensive the production process, learning effects are greatest in such sectors'.

The same point is made by Nelson:

> the learning of technology to the point of reasonable mastery is a highly active process, not a passive one ... Technology is not like a tennis racket which one can simply pick up at a store, pay for, and take home. Rather acquiring a technology is much more like acquiring the skills of playing tennis. One can buy 'tennis lessons', and that may help, but that is a far thing from actually buying the skills to play tennis well.

The ways in which a more open trade regime promotes productivity growth through learning effects are briefly described by Amsden:

> Learning effects don't depend upon increased production from trade *per se*, although trade may uniquely expose firms to new technological environments and consequently help them broaden their technological knowledge.

By opening up a channel to the world market, trade also serves to promote specialization and sustain production tempos of goods in which learning effects are embodied; if constrained by domestic mar-ket size along with associated domestic business cycle uncertainty of demand, firms would be less willing to make the investments needed to capture such learning effects.

The business management approach to the modelling of learning is summed up succinctly in Argote and Epple; this material is also briefly summarized in Amsden. Empirical work began with the observation in 1936 that unit labour costs in air-frame production declined with cu-mulative output. Subsequent case-studies have confirmed the existence of learning or experience effects in several industries and in a range of economic activities. Indeed, the evidence is that the potential for learning, and inevitably the costs of learning, rise quickly with increasing technological complexity. Learning associated with rising technical efficiency in a given technology, in the sense used in this chapter, is distinct from learning to use new technologies.

Learning is also not automatic, but strongly contingent upon various enabling conditions.[2] In general, learning is faster the more competitive the market environment, though it would logically seem that diminishing returns must set in at some point. It is also well known that knowledge accumulated in learning depreciates, just like physical capital. The rate of accumulation also depends on the frequency of employee turnover. Increasing exploitation of economies of scale seems to enhance learning, to some extent at least, but again there must be obvious limits; in any case the actual parameters are industry and technology specific.

These observations corroborate the remarks raised earlier on the distinctions between task efficiency and production management expertise. Amsden proposes a definition of skilled activity and a categorization of different skill classes. She supplements the conventional definition of skilled labour as raw labour enhanced by training and experience by noting that skill is a production factor that cannot yet be replaced by a machine within the margin of profitability. The progress of technology is hypothesized as successive stages in the automation of labour starting from the low-skill end. She notes that capital and skills are better treated as complements rather than substitutes in each stage in the short term. Progressive substitution then is a long-term effect.

Amsden defines skilled sectors as those that employ large numbers of skilled people. These sectors are considered conceptually and empirically distinct from sectors that employ large numbers of skilled people and large amounts of capital, or large amounts of capital and few skilled workers, or little capital and few skilled workers.

Productivity advance derives not only from individual learning by workers, skilled and otherwise. Amsden identifies learning achieved by organizations and also by the economy as a whole, all of which raise plant level productivity. This is an important insight further developed in Lall's writings on technological capability. The idea derives from the literature on technological change and institutional economics. Organizational learning is a well-documented phenomenon; it occurs as a concatenation of small, incremental improvements in technology or procedures that occur in the course of production.

Such incremental technological changes can be represented as downward shifts of the learning curve. It is generally greater the more skill-intensive the production process. Amsden argues that such adaptations and the learning effort elicited are greatest where the technology is least explicit, i.e., where it is not fully codified, not fully understood nor available in blueprint form. This seems to be where the greatest leeway for operational innovation exists. She gives examples of process plants in NICs where imported turnkey technology is incrementally adapted, by informal methods, to better perform with local raw materials, costs and conditions. While such effects occur to a limited extent in process industries, these are even more common in discrete batch or job-shop production processes.

Amsden's overarching point is as follows: the setting up and promotion, in NIC-type developing countries, of industries that are intensive in skill and/or capital has the important effect of raising human capital. This consideration is especially important when the producing country can export resulting capital goods output to other developing countries. South-South exports of skill-intensive goods can help to raise the stock of technological knowledge and skill levels in the exporting country. By contrast, resource-based South-North exports embody only a rent effect with little useful learning.

Notes

1. The material for this Appendix has been drawn from Amsden (1986, 1989), Argote and Epple (1990), Lall (1990), Nelson (1990), Pack (1987) and Rodrigo (1987, 1994).
2. Argote and Epple remark that Lockheed's production of the L-1011 Tri-Star aircraft in the 1970s is an example with little evidence of learning.

References

Amsden, Alice H. (1986), 'The Direction of Trade – Past and Present – And the "Learning Effects" of Exports to Different Directions', *Journal of Development Economics* 23(2), pp. 249–274.

Amsden, Alice H. (1989), *Asia's Next Giant: South Korea and Late Industrialization*, Oxford University Press, New York.

Argote, Linda and Dennis Epple (1990), 'Learning Curves in Manufacturing', *Science* 247, pp. 920–924.

Arrow, Kenneth J. (1991), *Returns to Scale, Information and Economic Growth*, Korea Development Institute Twentieth Anniversary Symposium on Economic Growth and Social Capability, Seoul, Republic of Korea.

Arthur, W. Brian (1990), 'Positive Feedbacks in the Economy', *Scientific American*, pp. 92–99.

Caves, Richard and David Barton (1990), *Efficiency in US Manufacturing Industries*, MIT Press, Cambridge MA.

Caves, Richard E. (ed.) (1992), *Industrial Efficiency in Six Nations*, MIT Press, Cambridge MA.

Dornbusch, Rudiger (1990), *Policies to Move from Stabilization to Growth*, Proceedings of the World Bank Annual Conference on Development Economics, World Bank, Washington, D.C.

Dornbusch, Rudiger (1993), 'The End of the German Miracle', *Journal of Economic Literature* 21, pp. 881–885.

Dosi, Giovanni, Christopher Freeman, Richard Nelson, Gerald Silverberg and Luc Soete (eds) (1988), *Technical Change and Economic Theory*, Pinter Publishers, London.

Krugman, Paul (1990), *Rethinking International Trade*, MIT Press, Cambridge MA.

Krugman, Paul (1991), 'History Versus Expectations', *Quarterly Journal of Economics* 106(2), pp. 651–667.

Krugman, Paul (1992), *Towards a Counter-Counter-Revolution in Development Theory*, World Bank Annual Conference on Development Economics, Washington, D.C.

Lall, Sanjaya (1990), *Building Industrial Competitiveness in Developing Countries*, OECD, Paris.

Lall, Sanjaya (1992), 'Technological Capabilities and Industrialization', *World Development* 20(2), pp. 165–186.

Lundvall, Bengt-Ake (ed.) (1992), *National Systems of Innovation: Towards a Theory of Innovation and Interactive Learning*, Pinter Publishers, London.

Nelson, Richard R. (1981), 'Research on Productivity Growth and Productivity Differences: Dead Ends and New Departures', *Journal of Economic Literature* 19, pp. 1029–1064.

Nelson, Richard R. (1990), 'Acquiring Technology', *Technological Challenge in the Asia-Pacific Economy*, Allen & Unwin, Sydney, Australia.

Nelson, Richard R. (1993), *National Innovation Systems: a Comparative Analysis*, Oxford University Press, New York.

North, Douglass C. (1989), 'Institutions and Economic Growth: An Historical Introduction', *World Development* 17(9), pp. 1319–1332.

Pack, Howard (1987), *Productivity, Technology and Industrial Development: a Case Study in Textiles*, World Bank/Oxford University Press, New York.

Pack, Howard (1988), 'Industrialization and Trade', *Handbook of Development Economics*, North-Holland, Amsterdam, pp. 334–380.

Pack, Howard (1992), 'New Perspectives on Industrial Growth in Taiwan', *Taiwan: from Developing to Mature Economy*, Westview Press, Boulder, CO, pp. 73–120.

Rodrigo, G. Chris (1987), *Development in Sri Lanka: Issues of Organization and Management*, South Asia Conference, University of Wisconsin, Madison.

Rodrigo, G. Chris (1994), *International Trade and the Sources of Growth: the Experience of East Asia*, Cornell University, Ithaca NY.

Rosenberg, Nathan (1982), *Inside the Black Box: Technology and Economics*, Cambridge University Press, Cambridge, United Kingdom.

Stiglitz, Joseph E. (1991), *Social Absorption Capability, Rent Seeking and Innovation*, Korea Development Institute Twentieth Anniversary Symposium on Economic Growth and Social Capability, Seoul, Republic of Korea.

Stiglitz, Joseph E. (1992), 'Comment on *Toward a Counter-Counter Revolution in Development Theory* by Krugman', World Bank Annual Conference on Development Economics, Washington, D.C.

Sah, Raaj Kumar and Joseph E. Stiglitz (1989), 'Sources of Technological Divergence Between Developed and Less Developed Countries', in *Debt, Stabilization and Development: Essays in Memory of Carlos Diaz-Alejandro*, Basil Blackwell Press, Oxford.

Summers, Robert and Alan Heston (1991), 'The Penn World Table (Mark 5.5): An Expanded Set of International Comparisons,1950–1988', *Quarterly Journal of Economics* 56, pp. 327–368.

Thorbecke, Erik (1990), 'Institutions, X-Efficiency, Transaction Costs and Socioeconomic Development', in *Studies in Economic Rationality: X-Efficiency Examined and Extolled*, University of Michigan Press, Ann Arbor, pp. 295–313.

Thorbecke, Erik (1991), 'The Indonesian Adjustment Experience in an International Perspective', Institute for Policy Reform, Washington, D.C.

Wade, Robert (1990), *Governing the Market: Economic Theory and the Role of Government in East Asian Industrialization*, Princeton University Press, Princeton, NJ.

World Bank (1992), *World Development Report*, Washington, D.C.

World Bank (1993), *The East Asian Miracle*, Oxford University Press, New York.

Young, Alwyn (1991), 'Learning by Doing and the Dynamic Effects of International Trade', *Quarterly Journal of Economics* 56(2), pp. 369–406.

Young, Alwyn (1992), 'A Tale of Two Cities: Factor Accumulation and Technical Change in Hong Kong and Singapore', *NBER Macroeconomics Annual 1992*, MIT Press, Cambridge MA, pp. 13–54.

2. Eastern European Lessons on Economic Restructuring: a Synthesis of the Literature

Konstantine Gatsios[*]

Introduction

Enterprise restructuring is about restoring efficiency in the employment and use of productive assets, capital and labour, thus providing incentives for innovation and growth. It involves changes in the ownership, control and organizational structures of enterprises. Usually it also involves changes in the economic environment within which enterprises operate.

Privatization of nationalized enterprises has often been associated with enterprise restructuring. The underlying idea is that industry performance will improve by strengthening the role of market forces. However, the ability of the latter in bringing about an efficient allocation of resources does not solely depend on privatization. It also requires additional measures that create a competitive environment. The promotion of competition by removing artificial restrictions on entry, by making resources equally available to potential entrants and by breaking down monopolies into several corporate entities are, arguably, the most effective means of attaining efficiency and growth, in restoring incentives for innovation and, hence, in maximizing consumer benefits.

While these are commonly accepted views, there is a substantive difference between industrial restructuring in western-type economies

[*]Athens University of Economics and Business, Athens; IMOII, Athens; and Centre for Economic Policy Research, London.

and in economies in transition like those in eastern Europe (EE). In the latter case, restructuring is a far more complex issue as it cannot be seen being independent from the transformation of the economic system as a whole. While, therefore, enterprise reform is the core economic problem in EE, it is at the same time part of a sweeping and far-reaching systemic change. As such it has to be treated in the context of, and in relation to, such issues as ensuring or restoring macroeconomic stability; the introduction of a new, rational set of prices; the development of well-functioning capital markets; and the creation of market-oriented incentives for management and workers.

Economic transformation has not only economic but also important political and social aspects. Political, because in economies in transition there are forces that would like to see the process of change being halted or even reversed. A traditional feature of centrally planned economies has been the concentration of the control of State assets, and therefore of wealth, in the hands of a largely uneducated and inexperienced State apparatus selected mainly according to political, as against professional, criteria. The members of the 'nomenklatura' thus created are likely to lose out from the successful completion of reforms and are, therefore, likely to resist it.

Economic reforms have also important social aspects. Maintaining popular support for completing the reform process is vital for its success. The transition process involves costs. None the less, it is of paramount importance that these costs should be distributed and seen to be distributed with fairness across the different groups of society. The population should not be marginalized from the reform process, which must result in as wide a structure of ownership as possible.

All this means that the decision-making process requires the active involvement of the main actors in the transformation process: the Government, the State agency responsible for restructuring and privatization, the banks, the existing enterprise management and the workers' unions. It is, therefore, essential that old institutions be restructured and new ones created in order to facilitate the attainment of the highest possible degree of social consensus concerning the nature and direction of changes. This is also important for the additional reason that during the transition period new problems not necessarily foreseen at the outset emerge and ought to be tackled quickly, decisively and successfully.

The following does not attempt to provide a detailed account of the transformation process in EE, but rather to draw some lessons that the experiences in these countries have taught us and to advance some suggestions, deemed to be relevant to economies in transition in general, not only to those of EE.

At a general level, a pervading lesson that can be drawn from EE points to the importance of the sequence and priorities of reform *vis-à-vis* the often overplayed distinction between 'shock therapy' and 'gradualism'.

The former German Democratic Republic offers the clearest example of shock therapy, which will be further detailed in Chapter 4. One cannot resist observing that despite the huge financial transfers from the West as well as the massive technical and administrative assistance provided, the spectre of creating a two-tier Germany has not been erased. At any rate, the case of the former German Democratic Republic is quite unique and hardly applicable elsewhere in eastern Europe.

On the other hand, Hungary is the most representative example of gradualism. But then, unlike the rest of EE countries, Hungary could draw on two decades of prior economic reforms which progressively introduced market economic institutions. Hungary was the first country in the region to allow corporate or private businesses to be established, mostly in services but also in small-scale industry, agriculture and construction, providing goods and services either to the wider public or to the large State-owned enterprises (SOEs). Under the 1988 Enterprise Law, most of these businesses became limited liability companies. Consequently, in Hungary the legal procedures for establishing a firm had been in operation well before the regime change. In short, shock therapy was not undertaken because it was not needed. On the contrary, Hungary's tradition laid the foundation for a gradual transition to a market economy.

Tax Reform

Turning to more specific issues, the first lesson from EE experiences relates to the importance, especially for economies in transition, of a modern and efficiently administered tax system. A common experience of all EE countries has been a sharp decline in output following the regime change. Whatever the possible statistical measurement errors may be, there is little doubt that the economies of these countries are undergoing a severe depression. To some extent this is due to the stabilization measures *per se* and, arguably, to improper sequencing of reforms as the high costs of freeing foreign trade ahead of structural reforms at the enterprise level, the excessive currency undervaluations resulting in a sharp fall in real wages and a negative demand shock, as well as the neglect of the large State sector. Moreover, the collapse of intra-CMEA trade, and especially of trade with the independent States that were republics of the former USSR, was also clearly very painful. On the other hand, the stabilization programmes undertaken made visible what was in fact a hidden depression – that is, hidden unemployment, hidden inflation, unviable firms and activities generating negative value-added. In this respect, depression was to some extent unavoidable.

In turn, the fall in output triggered an acute fiscal crisis. This made macroeconomic management extremely difficult. The root of the crisis can be traced to the fact that EE Governments relied primarily on SOE profits as a source of revenue. With the fall in output and the decline in SOE profitability, the tax base eroded rapidly. Furthermore, the transfer of some SOEs into the private sector increased difficulties – and will continue doing so in the future – since newly privatized firms usually enjoy tax privileges.

At the same time, rising unemployment increased government expenditure for unemployment benefits. Often over-generous social provisions have also contributed to raising public expenditure. In addition, for countries like Hungary with high foreign debt, the fiscal burden of its service has been quite heavy.

Because financial markets in EE are underdeveloped, deficits tend to be monetized. This entails monetary expansion and crowding out of investment. It is, therefore, extremely important for these countries to strengthen their budgetary discipline by controlling public spending, ensuring adequate tax revenues and keeping the two roughly in balance.

The development of a modern tax system and its efficient administration is, therefore, of first order importance. Western technical assistance in this respect is valuable. The value-added tax and the personal income tax should be the key instruments of such a tax system, while taxes on corporate profits should be of much less importance. In fact, it is essential that firms are provided with incentives to reinvest their profits. As will be discussed later, fiscal considerations consist of an additional reason for avoiding the free disposal of State assets.

Tax reform is also important for political and social reasons. The black or grey economy that has developed in EE countries, especially in Hungary, might have been a source of supply-side flexibility, but it has also contributed to a weak tax morality. It is important that measures should be taken to counter tax evasion and ensure that the costs of economic reforms are widely and fairly distributed. Social justice is vital in achieving consensus on economic reforms.

In the same spirit, subsidies to loss-making firms should be reduced or cut in the context of a conscious and coherent industrial policy. In any case, they should be on an explicit cash-limited form, so that firms start facing hard budget constraints. Cuts on infrastructure, education and health should, on the other hand, be as minimal as possible. These are areas that have been underfunded under the previous regimes and their further deterioration could have very adverse social and political effects.

It is perhaps useful to cite here the Hungarian experience. In Hungary, a tax-on-profit regime was introduced in 1968. It superseded the disastrous practice of appropriating for the State's treasury all corporate profits in excess of their planned levels, a policy amounting to a 100-per-cent marginal tax rate. Additionally, a value-added tax and a personal income tax were introduced in 1988. Arguably, these policies were more a result of outside pressure (especially from the World Bank and IMF) rather than the outcome of a conscious attempt to introduce a western-type system of taxation. It is not surprising, therefore, that they were full of contradictions. For instance, the simultaneous introduction of special, firm-specific taxes and subsidies devised to skim income from healthy, profitable firms and to use the proceeds to support unprofitable enterprises, manifested the reluctance of the central authorities to let firms freely use their after-tax profits, and it completely offset the effect of value-added tax on resource allocation. Similarly, the direct control of personal income in the State sector negated the introduction of the personal income tax.

However – and this is the important point – having a modern tax system in place gave Hungary a great advantage over other countries in the region. What was needed to be done was the removal of the distortions inhibiting the operation of this tax system, and this was implemented fairly rapidly after the regime change. In this sense, Hungary was fortunate. It could dismantle the old tax/subsidy system without dangerously jeopardizing government revenues. It is widely accepted that the existence of a modern tax system in Hungary has been an important prerequisite for its relatively strong and steady revenues, even in the face of recession, and for its moderate inflation rates.

Trade Policy Reforms

A second lesson relates to trade policy and demonopolization. In EE, the opening of trade with the West – together with currency convertibility, low tariffs and limited quantitative restrictions on imports – was too abrupt and it amplified the initial shock. Despite the initial devaluations in the Czech Republic, Poland and Slovakia, many important industries became vulnerable.

Trade liberalization should be gradual and proceed in pace with domestic liberalization and demonopolization. The main argument for liberalizing foreign trade is that it represents a quick way of establishing sensible prices and of putting the traded sector under competitive pressure. This, combined with hard budget constraints, could force enterprises to behave more efficiently in their use of resources and choice of investment.

While this argument is in principle correct, one should not forget that many of the inefficiencies of centrally planned economies were linked to their bias towards large firms and monopolized production structures, which make soft budget constraints almost inevitable. Hence, trade liberalization without demonopolization and restructuring may be insufficient to guarantee productive efficiency. There are at least three reasons for this:

- The first reason is that trade liberalization has *little effect on the non-traded sectors* in terms of introducing competitive pressures. At the same time, many of these sectors (such as transport and services) are inputs into the traded goods sectors. If, therefore, they are not forced to become more efficient by liberalization and exposure to entry, then the traded goods sectors will not be able to successfully adjust to competitive pressures from abroad and may be unduly hurt. Furthermore, if foreign imports remain in the hands of monopoly distribution networks, then market liberalization will be seriously compromised.
- The second reason has to do with the fact that many SOEs, both in the traded and non-traded sectors, are *vertically or horizontally*

integrated conglomerates, producing too wide a variety of goods. This makes it difficult to determine which lines of business are profitable, as cross-subsidization allows unviable units to survive, distorting in this way the signals for restructuring. As a result, firms that may be unprofitable at world prices could, if restructured, generate positive value-added and net profits. The danger, therefore, of instant trade liberalization is to put many of these firms out of business, together with those that are unviable.

* The third reason is that the probability of *capture of regulators or politicians* is higher in concentrated industries. They are better placed to lobby for protection such as quotas or to pressure for an undervalued exchange rate (i.e., low real wages) in order to protect their inefficient production. If successful, this would mean that the efficiency results intended by trade liberalization may be offset, at least partially.

Demonopolization is, therefore, an essential component of the reform process towards an efficient market economy. Breaking large conglomerates into smaller units and removing barriers to entry results in increased market competition, provides performance standards against which firms can be measured and, hence, facilitates the allocation of credit. During this restructuring process, tariffs may temporarily safeguard some efficiently produced output and employment.

It is probably equally important that Governments can credibly commit themselves to a policy of trade liberalization for a definite near future and that enterprise restructuring can be seen as the reason, not the pretext, for not instantly liberalizing imports. In this context, it is advisable that Governments proceed to currency convertibility as soon as possible, ahead of trade liberalization. Convertibility, accompanied by a sensible exchange rate policy that avoids excessive initial devaluations, establishes to a significant extent the credibility of openness as it increases competition with imported goods and establishes a new equilibrium price structure.

Enterprise Reform

The third lesson from EE experiences relates to enterprise reform. This is the core problem in transforming centrally planned economies into market economies. A common characteristic, at least in the initial phases of the regime change in EE, has been an aversion to anything like industrial policies. This aversion might have been a consequence of previous centralized planning and a reaction to it. None the less, it had painful consequences. It resulted in 'State desertion', which in the name of *laissez-faire* pushed State enterprises adrift, operating under weak, often perverse, incentives and no central guidance. Part of the decline in industrial output in EE countries has to be attributed to State neglect of the large public sector. It needs to be understood that the market cannot, and will not, restructure the large SOEs – and most of them are too big to fail. Even when they are broken up and bankruptcy does become possible, restructuring will need guidance. In circumstances of economies in radical transformation, short-run profitability may be a distorted indicator of the actual capacity of a firm to restructure and survive.

Clearly, it is not possible to run an enterprise efficiently if its ownership and control are in limbo. Hence, a clarification of medium-term ownership should be the starting point of any restructuring plan. Similarly, clear assignment of control rights over the enterprises need to be established immediately to avoid destructive power feuds, which often lead to the decapitalization of firms.

To achieve clarification of ownership status, the first necessary decision is which firms are to be eventually privatized and which are to remain in State hands even in the long run. In the latter case, the companies should be transferred to a separate agency that will deal with those enterprises that are to remain in State ownership; the State as senior creditor and owner can afterwards establish their scheme of governance. The incentive problems in permanent State enterprises are entirely different from those faced in enterprises about to be privatized and are not different from those in developed, western-type economies. Thus, the concentration here will be on the enterprises to be privatized.

Those firms need to be commercialized immediately and to be provided with a proper legal framework (such as joint-stock companies). At the same time, large vertically and horizontally integrated conglomerates should be broken down (demonopolization) whenever possible, and managers should be given appropriate incentives that stop the decapitalization of the State firms and induce them to reorganize and to seek new markets. Finally, privatization should be pursued with a wide menu of methods adapted to political, economic and industrial circumstances.

Each one of the five EE countries has opted for a different privatization programme. Among the many distinctions that can be drawn between these five programmes, one concerns the fact that two countries have chosen a strategy of piecemeal sale of assets (Germany and Hungary) while the three others (Czech Republic, Poland and Slovakia) have favoured mass privatization programmes with give-away schemes.

At a political level, free distribution schemes have the important advantage of creating a large constituency in favour of privatization reforms, a counter-thrusting force against vested interests opposed to the privatization process.

At an economic level, the real advantage of give-away schemes is speed, although just how much time such schemes can save is far from clear. Even if the valuation stage can be bypassed, there are still important decisions to be made (such as restructuring financial debts, producing opening balance sheets, transforming enterprises into joint-stock companies) that make plans of quick privatization impossible. Evidence to date does not indicate that privatization in countries that have opted for such schemes has been any faster for that.

The main drawback of give-away schemes is their budgetary impact and the consequent unleash of inflation. As mentioned earlier, all EE countries were faced with a fiscal crisis and a rather underdeveloped tax system (with the exception of Hungary). Since the development of a modern tax system takes time, one of the main priorities in these countries, together with demonopolization and the creation of a competitive environment, should be the maximization of proceeds from the sale of State assets. Even if the pursuit of this objective may go against accelerating the pace of privatization, this is a small price to pay for the guarantee of a smooth transition process.

Another drawback of mass privatization is that incumbent management is left in place at the moment of privatization and no satisfactory procedure is set up to remove inefficient staff and replace them with more competent professionals.

State assets should, therefore, not be given away but sold – and preferably through auctions. Sales privatization, however, faces two problems. The first concerns the valuation of assets in the absence of capital markets. The second and most serious one concerns the so-called 'stock-flow' constraint. That is, without pre-existing private wealth or capital markets, the most the Government can get from selling the stock of State assets is the flow of savings. The latter, though, cannot quickly absorb the former.

A useful, though not perfect, method which has been suggested to resolve both these problems is for the Government or privatization agency to organize auctions where potential buyers can submit both cash and non-cash bids. The latter involve the transfer of control into private hands in exchange for debt claims or other securities, thus transforming the Government into a net nominal creditor. The types of non-cash bids can be standard debt, voting shares (common stock), non-voting shares (preferred stock), leasing contracts and management buy-outs.

This method of privatization has the advantage that, in principle, the Government can accelerate the pace of privatization without substantially reducing the total proceeds from the sale of State assets. It also has a desirable macroeconomic property: since the Government is turned into a nominal creditor, it introduces an anti-inflationary bias into the economy.

But most importantly, the advantage of non-cash bids is that many (potential) buyers with little current wealth can bid for State assets by committing either to sharing future revenues with the State or to future debt repayment to the State. Since, therefore, the non-cash bids reflect the bidders' willingness, rather than merely ability, to pay, and since this willingness to pay in turn reflects their ability to profitably run an enterprise, this method of privatization leads to greater production efficiency. It achieves a better management-to-assets match. In addition, incompetent but wealthy 'nomenklatura' members will be in a less favourable position to outbid less affluent but more competent buyers.

Another desirable property of the scheme of cash and non-cash bids is that it introduces capital markets. It also allows the Government to write off the existing enterprise debt without substantial revenue loss, since the debt write-offs will be reflected in higher bids for the State firms. An important additional advantage of cancelling outstanding debt before privatization is that the Government will not be faced in the future with the prospect of writing off some of these debts in firms that have inherited an unusually high amount of debt, thus raising doubts in the minds of managers as to its commitment to enforce debt repayment.

Perhaps such auctions are easier to organize for small or medium-sized firms where it makes sense to have managers-owners and a reasonably concentrated ownership structure. The privatization of larger firms is likely to bring about a separation of ownership and control, as the winning bidders will own but a small fraction of the cash-flow claims. In this case, what is in fact auctioned is managerial positions and, consequently, identifying serious buyers and monitoring the firms' management may need to be done either by supervisory boards, like those in Germany, or by the banks.

The Role of the Financial Sector

The fourth lesson concerns the role of the financial sector. Western loan-classification practices show that most of the banks in EE that have spun off from the central mono-bank are, in fact, insolvent. This is because of the large burden of debt that SOEs carry and cannot service. Consequently, the main commercial banks, which are the major creditors of SOEs, have large amounts of virtually worthless paper dominating their assets portfolio. Clearly, therefore, a separate treatment of enterprise debt and bank recapitalization is impossible. A successful restructuring plan needs to address both problems jointly.

While banks are severely undercapitalized, suffer from exclusive non-performing loans and face political pressures to finance struggling SOEs, they may plausibly conclude, on the basis of experience, that their debtors are too big to fail and will eventually be rescued by the State budget. This creates creditor passivity by the banks which, in turn, reinforces inter-enterprise creditor passivity. More importantly, it creates an interlocking network of banks and enterprises that may indeed, in aggregate, become too big to fail and which in effect redistributes liquidity from sound to potentially unviable enterprises. Furthermore, the refinancing of incumbents impedes entry and suspends exit.

The market cannot and will not work if credit markets do not function. Moreover, when there are major credit market failures, restructuring and privatization alone are unlikely to promote substantially greater efficiency.

It is, therefore, essential in the context of a banking reform to recapitalize banks with enough income-earning assets to leave a prudential capital base in place after making provisions for bad loans. Only then will financial discipline be possible and capital markets can operate.

Recapitalization through a prolonged period of high spreads between lending and borrowing rates is inefficient. It works by taxing successful firms to fund the losses of unsuccessful ones, thus inhibiting growth. A once-off capital infusion based on public debt issue would allow for a less destructive way of financing the resulting liabilities.

In this way, banks can also act as agents of change. This is desirable since they are better placed than others to judge the potential of a client firm and the merits of a restructuring plan. Of course, converting much bank debt into equity causes regulatory problems since it is difficult to evaluate the equity for capital adequacy calculations, as equity is likely to remain non-traded in most cases. However, it creates at the same time a concentrated ownership that has one big advantage: at least there will be a group of shareholders that will have the incentives and the ability to actively monitor managers. This is particularly important in the case of large firms for which, as mentioned before, only a limited part of the shares will pass to winning bidders and where there will therefore be a separation between ownership and control. It should be noted that the regulatory problem is likely to be minor for some time if banks are recapitalized upfront on the basis of a conservative assessment of the status of the loans to be converted into equity. As time goes by and the regulatory problem grows, the banks can be made gradually to sell off the equity. To avoid the fire-sale problems associated with instantaneous liquidation, a substantial time period (about five years) should be allowed for this.

Not to have taken immediate and comprehensive action in restructuring their financial system has been one of the most important errors in the sequencing of the reforms in EE, with a huge cost to enterprise restructuring and to output.

The Czech Republic and Hungary have recently taken limited measures to recapitalize their banks and to deal with the overhang of enterprise debt. The Government of Poland has obtained World Bank assistance to support a plan for partial recapitalization of the banks and reduction of enterprise debts.

Income Policies

The final lesson relates to income policies. In the turmoil and uncertainties of economic transformation, it is important to try to maintain the stability of real wages at a realistic level through formal and informal income policies. Hungary has been the most successful of EE countries in establishing such an informal social pact. An abrupt fall in real wages, prompted for instance through an excessive devaluation, should be avoided. While in a growing economy lower real wages can provide a competitive edge in the production of tradeables and can stimulate investment demand, in a declining economy an abrupt fall in real wages is simply a negative demand shock, while its reversal may be inflationary. This was the experience in Poland in 1990 and in the former Czechoslovakia in 1991.

However, stability of real wages will not be possible unless growing unemployment is cushioned by an effective social safety net and labour market institutions. Modern trade unions have a responsibility here in the implementation of income policies and the development of the social safety net.

References

Bibliographic note

This paper is based on a wide range of literature on eastern Europe developed over the past five years. Because of its synthetic nature, explicit references have been omitted in the text and replaced by a bibliography which the interested reader might want to explore further. In particular, Portes (1993) presents a good survey of country cases as well as a synopsis of the problems today facing the eastern European countries. The reader interested in the Hungarian case should look at Gatsios (1992) and Hare and Revesz (1992) and the references therein, whereas Carlin and Mayer (1992) is recommended for the case of the former German Democratic Republic, despite the reservations one might have regarding their conclusions. The privatization method using cash and non-cash bids has been proposed by Boldon and Roland (1992) and is highly recommended. For the opposite privatization method involving mass transfers of State property with the use of give-away schemes, the interested reader should look at Lipton and Sachs (1990) and Blanchard et al. (1991). Sweder van Wijnbergen (1992) provides an excellent discussion of enterprise as well as bank reform in eastern Europe. For the issue of bankruptcy reform and its relation to the transition to a market economy, the interested reader could start by looking at Abel and Gatsios (1993) and Aghion et al. (1992). Finally, Newbery (1991 *a* and *b*) provides a compelling argument for the demonopolization of EE economies as a prerequisite for liberalization.

Abel, I. and K. Gatsios (1993), 'The Economics of Bankruptcy and the Transition to a Market Economy', *CEPR Discussion Paper 878*, CEPR, London.

Aghion, P. and R. Burgess (1992), 'Financing and Development in Eastern Europe and the Former Soviet Union', *LSE Financial Markets Group Special Paper 46*, LSE, London.

Aghion, P., O. Hart and J. Moore (1992), 'The Economics of Bankruptcy Reform' in O. Blanchard and K. Froot (eds): *Transition in Eastern Europe*, NBER.

Begg, D. (1991), 'Economic Reform in Czechoslovakia: Should We Believe in Santa Klaus?' *Economic Policy*.

Begg, D. and R. Portes (1992), 'Enterprise Debt and Economic Transformation: Financial Restructuring of the State Sector in Central and Eastern Europe', *CEPR Discussion Paper 695*, CEPR, London.

Blanchard, O., R. Dornbusch, P. Krugman, R. Layard and L. Summers (1991), *Reform in Eastern Europe*, MIT Press, Cambridge, MA.

Bofinger, P. and I. Cernohorsky (1992), 'Some Lessons from Economic Transformation in East Germany', *CEPR Discussion Paper 686*, CEPR, London.

Boldon, P. and G. Roland (1992), 'Privatization in Central and Eastern Europe', *Economic Policy*.

Carlin, W. and C. Mayer (1992), 'Enterprise Restructuring', *Economic Policy*.

Dervis, K. and T. Gordon (1992), 'Hungary: An Emerging Gradualist Success Story?' in O. Blanchard and K. Froot (eds) *Transition in Eastern Europe*, NBER.

Frydman, K. and A. Rapaczynski (1990), 'Markets and Institutions in Large Scale Privatizations' in V. Corbo and F. Coricelli (eds) *Adjustment and Growth: Lessons for Eastern Europe*, World Bank.

Gatsios, K. (1992), 'Privatization in Hungary: Past, Present and Future', *CEPR Discussion Paper 642*, CEPR, London.

Grosfeld, I. and P. Hare (1991), 'Privatization in Hungary, Poland and Czechoslovakia', *European Economy*.

Hamilton, C. and L. A. Winters (1992), 'Opening Up International Trade in Eastern Europe', *Economic Policy*.

Hare, P. and T. Revesz (1992), 'Hungary', *Economic Policy*.

Hughes, G. and P. G. Hare (1991), 'Competitiveness and Industrial Restructuring in Czechoslovakia, Hungary and Poland', *European Economy*.

Kornai, J. (1986), 'The Soft Budget Constraint', *Kyklos*.

Lipton, D. and J. Sachs (1990), 'Privatization in Eastern Europe: The Case of Poland', *Brookings Papers on Economic Activity*.

Mayhew, K. and P. Seabright (1992), 'Incentives and the Management of Enterprises in Economic Transition: Capital Markets are not Enough', *CEPR Discussion Paper 640*, CEPR, London.

Newbery, D. M. (1991/a), 'Reform in Hungary: Sequencing and Privatization', *European Economic Review*.

Newbery, D. M. (1991/b), 'Sequencing the Transition', *CEPR Discussion Paper 575*, CEPR, London.

Portes, R. (ed.) (1993), *Economic Transformation in Central Europe: A Progress Report*, CEPR, London.

Roland, G. and T. Verdier (1991), 'Privatization in Eastern Europe: Irreversibility and Critical Mass Effects', *CEPR Discussion Paper 612*, CEPR, London.

Szekely, I. (1990), 'The Reform of the Hungarian Financial System', *European Economy*.

Tirole, J. (1991), 'Privatization in Eastern Europe: Incentives and the Economics of Transition', *Macroeconomics Annual*, NBER.

Wijnbergen, S. van (1992), 'Enterprise Reform in Eastern Europe', *CEPR Discussion Paper 738*, CEPR, London.

3. Restructuring of Public Enterprises and Privatization

*Nilgün Gökgür**

Introduction

As the policy makers work to fashion industrial strategies, they will do well to consider recent efforts of developing countries in Latin America, Asia, Africa, and more recently in eastern and central Europe.[1] At least since 1985, the efforts in developing countries have largely focused on restructuring of public enterprises and privatization in conjunction with macroeconomic stabilization and liberalization programmes. Distressed by the poor performance of their public enterprise sector, Governments hoped to achieve competitiveness in international markets through private entrepreneurship, innovation and better performing public enterprises.

However, attempts to restructure and privatize yielded mixed results. While it is impossible to predict success with any degree of assurance, it is possible to identify some of those factors that seem to have facilitated overall restructuring and privatization programmes. The successful programmes did not come without difficulties. Governments, who managed and monitored desirable outcomes, were skilled in dealing with all the obstacles encountered during the implementation phase of these programmes. The purpose of this chapter is to review the factors promoting successful restructuring and privatization programmes, to identify the obstacles encountered, to provide examples of overcoming them, and to summarize the means, methods and modalities utilized.

*Harvard Business School, Cambridge, MA and Boston Institute for Developing Economies.

Impetus for Restructuring and Privatization

As was the case with the United Kingdom, which became the pace-setter for many developed and developing countries in the early 1980s, much of the impetus for restructuring and privatization came from the evident failure of public enterprises. Even more than in the United Kingdom, public enterprise had become the predominant mode of economic activity in the developing world.

During the 1960s, many newly independent countries in Africa either inherited certain public enterprises or nationalized the private firms previously owned by their colonizers. Even in the absence of former colonial relationships at the time, many Latin American and Asian countries simply chose to take over the multinational corporations to strengthen their national sovereignty. Furthermore, public enterprise was fostered as a way to rescue private enterprise that was faltering. They were also established as a way of promoting new capital formation, creating jobs and advancing equity among socio-economic (and ethnic) groups and regions.

By the early 1980s, however, it was already clear that public enterprises were neither making profits nor fulfilling the social objectives of increased equity, investment and employment. The reasons for their failure were too easy to identify: unclear, multiple and contradictory objectives, bureaucratic interference, overly centralized decision-making, managerial ineptitude, excessive personnel costs, high labour turnover and price controls all undermined the efficiency and the profitability of public enterprises.

Consequently, loss-making and heavy indebtedness increasingly began to impose a financial burden on governments' budgets, and on the banking system. The net financial flows from the Government to public enterprises on average amounted to as much as two thirds of the national Government's budget deficit, and in some countries represented up to 10 per cent of the gross domestic product. Heavily indebted public enterprises often failed to pay back their loans. The private sector also suffered from the shortage of credit required for its own needs and expansion.

Not surprisingly, poorly performing public enterprises became a major impediment to economic growth and to international economic competitiveness. They failed to respond to the changing competitive dynamics of the world economy which called for more flexibility. For many developing countries, possible alternatives became clear. Countries in East and South-East Asia emerged with advantages in costs, productivity and government support. Their exports of manufactured products had replaced the exports of traditional commodities in generating sufficient revenue to finance growing imports. Moreover, the international competitiveness achieved by the countries in East and South-East Asia was no longer based on price. Quality, product differentiation, delivery time, marketing, before- and after-sales services and capacity to adopt to user needs became increasingly crucial for capturing international markets.

More specifically, the example of the countries in East and South-East Asia (and, to a lesser extent, of Latin America) showed the possibilities of success based on revealed comparative advantage (RCA).[2] Between 1967 and 1987, the second tier of Asian countries (Indonesia, Malaysia and Thailand) took over the RCA in industries from the first tier Asian countries (China (Taiwan Province), Hong Kong, Republic of Korea and Singapore). The first tier increasingly lost revealed comparative advantage to second tier Asian countries in labour-intensive industries while improving its RCAs in more technology- and high skill-intensive industries. Indonesia managed to take over the RCA from the first tier in industries such as cotton fabrics, woven textiles, clothing, veneers, plywood and shaped wood. Malaysia took over the RCA from the first tier in industries such as vegetable oils, clothing and woven textiles. Thailand captured the RCA from the first tier in industries such as preserved fruits and canned fish.[3]

Not only the Governments themselves, but also the major international organizations recognized these alternatives. The World Bank and IMF insisted on reform packages to help developing countries catch up with one another's rapidly growing penetration into international markets. The immediate set of policies included import and export liberalization and macroeconomic stabilization. Restructuring to streamline the performance of their public enterprises and privatization became an essential component of these reform packages, and even a precondition for numerous structural adjustment loans and stand-by agreements.

Objectives of Public Enterprise Restructuring and Privatization

As the problems associated with the performance of public enterprises became widely acknowledged, many Governments first tried standard public enterprise reforms (decentralization, giving enterprises more autonomy, elimination of government subsidies, obligation to pay taxes, etc.). They soon came to the realization that these reforms alone were not sufficient. New measures to restructure and privatize ownership were the only way to guarantee better performance of these enterprises. Some Governments, therefore, utilized restructuring at the enterprise level as an intermediate step prior to privatization. Some, on the other hand, chose a combined approach. They restructured some enterprises without change of ownership while simultaneously preparing others for sale.

The shared primary goal of both restructuring and privatization was to improve enterprise efficiency and to achieve higher economic growth. Exposing restructured public enterprises to the discipline of the market economy was to increase both efficiency and productivity. Improved performance thus would eliminate both the fiscal and administrative burden on the Government's budget and on internal and external debt, while increasing investment and employment.

Where restructuring led to privatization with change of ownership, Governments tried to fulfil other additional objectives: *(a)* to raise revenue for the Government through the sale price; *(b)* to deepen and extend the capital markets; *(c)* to stimulate local entrepreneurship and increase investments and employment; *(d)* to strengthen competitiveness in international markets through the exports of manufactured goods; and *(e)* to ensure equitable distribution of ownership, wealth and income among different socio-economic and ethnic groups and regions.

However, the objective of reaching equitable distribution of ownership often conflicted with efficiency – the primary goal of many restructuring and privatization programmes. The most successful programmes recognized this conflict at the outset and managed to sort it out. They were ultimately committed not to forgo efficiency under any circumstances. After all, only the efficient enterprises achieved growth, increased productivity, investments and, therefore, employment in the long run.

Factors Promoting Successful Restructuring Programmes and Privatization

All successful restructuring and privatization programmes relied on four common factors as outlined below. First, these programmes only succeeded in the presence of a competitive economic environment and capital markets. Second, they needed a well-functioning legal and regulatory framework. Third, they were best monitored and implemented by dedicated institutions, specifically established for that purpose. Fourth, both the Governments and these dedicated institutions defined their programme objectives clearly and communicated them to the general public.

- *Creation of a competitive economic environment and capital markets*

    Restructuring and privatization programmes succeeded in creating a competitive economic environment. Enterprise efficiency and productivity only increased as long as the newly restructured and privatized enterprises could operate in markets open to competition. These markets were established by macroeconomic reforms such as exchange rate, fiscal, trade and price reforms. Also, private sector development required a well-functioning banking sector. Capital markets were also needed, especially for privatization transactions that utilized public offerings. Some Governments specifically used public offerings as a privatization method in order to create or simply revitalize their capital markets. Argentina's and Mexico's privatization of telecommunications companies (ENTEL and TELEMEX, respectively) have served this purpose.[4]

    Furthermore, capital markets became critical in attracting portfolio equity investments from industrialized nations in North America, western Europe and Japan. These investments grew from US$ 3.5 billion in 1989 to US$ 13.2 billion in 1993 (US$ 30 billion were projected for 1994). However, only the Latin American, Asian, and eastern and southern European stock markets became the beneficiaries of these flows, which came either from the institutional investors and managed funds or in the form of returning capital flight. Domestic residents (as well as non-resident nationals) of developing countries with overseas holdings became significant individual investors in these emerging stock markets.[5] Even though the privatization processes of ENTEL and TELEMEX had first relied on private offerings, the subsequent flotations attracted the return of flight capital to their respective stock markets.[6]

• *Establishment of legal and regulatory framework*

A sound legal framework became necessary for the enforcement of the basic business laws, land, company, bankruptcy and contract. In certain cases, Governments revised the customary laws and, if necessary, created new ones in order to establish a well-defined set of property rights. This became crucial in countries like Madagascar, where businessmen needed to prove ownership of land and other assets to receive commercial credit from the banks.[7]

At the same time, successful restructuring and privatization programmes did not fail to take the precautionary measures for the long term. Especially in the case of privatizing the natural monopolies, Governments recognized far in advance the need for a regulatory framework to protect the interests of the consumers after transfer of the enterprise to the private sector. In the absence of a regulatory framework, the new private owners tended to operate the enterprise as a monopoly with, subsequently, a loss of consumer welfare.

• *Creation of dedicated institutions and careful planning*

Several Governments created dedicated institutions to monitor and implement restructuring and privatization programmes. These institutions were given the task of analysing the public enterprise portfolio which included all parastatals – departmental enterprises, wholly government-owned public stock companies and mixed enterprises (joint-stock companies). Once the total public enterprise portfolio was assessed, and the issues of each sector and the enterprises were identified, the governmental body in charge selected the methods and modalities for restructuring each enterprise. The sequence and pace of restructuring differed from country to country and from enterprise to enterprise.

Some Governments became overly cautious in the planning stage. They enlisted the services of international merchant banks to prepare the so-called 'privatization master plans'. While the Government of Turkey called upon the Morgan Guaranty Trust in 1985, the Government of Malaysia selected a British Merchant Bank (J. Henry Schroder Wagg) jointly with the Arab Malaysian

Merchant Bank in 1988. Both countries individually spent over US$ 2 million for these plans alone. However, there was no correlation between the amount of money spent and the pace of the programme. Turkey and Malaysia each experienced a different pace in their efforts to privatize according to the recommendations in the master plans. While the Turkish political leaders failed to sustain the necessary political support for privatization, the Malaysian authorities remained more determined and, therefore, more successful.

• *Setting and communicating programme objectives*

Clear definition of restructuring and privatization objectives not only helped build a consensus at the outset, but it also determined the political and social support in the long run. These objectives had to be communicated to the key economic actors – the public enterprise managers, employees, workers, private businessmen, consumers, creditors, competitors, all government ministries and agencies, as well as the general public. Some Governments achieved this with the national appeal of their charismatic leaders (Prime Minister Mahathir Mohamad in Malaysia, President Turgut Ozal in Turkey). Others, on the other hand, relied heavily on nationwide public awareness programmes through the media (Nigeria and Tunisia).

In Malaysia, it was first the Government that clarified its objectives prior to the establishment of a dedicated institution. The restructuring and privatization programme began as part of the Government's overall industrialization policy towards 'Malaysia Incorporated'. This concept viewed the country as a corporate entity and defined a new role for the Government as providing the macroeconomic policy support, while the private sector would contribute commercial and managerial expertise. The Government articulated in detail its objectives and the expected processes in Guidelines on Privatization. The Guidelines helped clarify the Government's plan to the wider community, including the private sector, while at the same time ensuring transparency. Only after the issuance of the guidelines did the Government establish the Privatization Committee under the chairmanship of the Economic Planning Unit (EPU) within the office of the Prime Minister.[8]

The Central Privatization Commission in Mexico was first given full authority to design the disengagement programme, and subsequently to spell out the Government's objectives.[9] The same objective was also articulated repeatedly by President Salinas. Every political statement stressed efficiency enhancement as the principal goal of Mexican divestiture and was broadly communicated as such.

In a move quite akin to Mexico's, the Government of Turkey created in 1987 the Public Participation Fund to implement its privatization programme. This agency dedicated to restructuring and privatization was given the mandate to update the privatization master plan, prepared a year earlier by Morgan Guaranty Trust. In addition, it had to identify the candidates for privatization under the privatization law.

The approach used by the Government of Nigeria was not much different. It also created by decree a similar high-level committee, the Technical Committee on Privatization and Commercialization (TCPC), with full authority for implementing its programme. The TCPC secretariat was staffed by professionals from the private sector. They were well paid and motivated. The Government of Tunisia achieved this goal by setting up a privatization ministry to implement its privatization programme. Both the Governments of Nigeria and Tunisia launched effective public awareness campaigns. These campaigns through the press and media helped the public understand why they should support the government programme, how they could participate in it, and what they were to gain (or to lose) from it.

Obstacles to Successful Restructuring and Privatization

Despite their overwhelming success, restructuring and privatization programmes proved to be a difficult process in many developing countries. They were more difficult in countries where there was virtually no private sector to begin with and the economic environment was not market friendly. The level of the difficulty also varied with the type of public enterprises that were restructured and divested. The enterprises in the competitive sectors were much easier to privatize than the natural monopolies.

The restructuring and privatization programmes were not only difficult, but costly as well. In the first place, they were politically costly because the Government had to overcome the existing bias in favour of keeping the public enterprises in the State sector. Even though they managed to draw political support in the beginning, political certainty and continuity were essential. Secondly, they became economically costly because their implementation necessitated the allocation of the Government's scarce economic resources and talent to this activity. Furthermore, social safety nets, severance payments and allocation of shares to employees or workers at low prices, imposed an additional burden to the Government's already tight budget.

Some countries established a special fund to cover the cost of restructuring and privatization. Malaysia's special fund helped to finance such expenses as feasibility studies, to prepare candidates for privatization and to disburse compensation related to privatization. Some took cost-cutting measures in financing the overall cost of these programmes. Mexico and Nigeria made full use of independent expertise available at home, including merchant banks and issuance houses, accounting and legal firms, and general management consulting firms. Mexico utilized international expertise whenever necessary.

While the costs of restructuring and privatization were obvious to all concerned, their overall benefits none the less remained for a large part invisible. First of all, they were often poorly understood among the policy makers themselves. Secondly, they were not widely communicated to the general public. Only recently, a group of academics at Boston University[10] analysed, on behalf of the World Bank, the welfare gains after the privatization in 12 companies in four countries (Chile, Mexico, Malaysia and the United Kingdom – the latter as the pace-setter for all other countries). The companies selected were mostly natural monopolies such as telecommunications, electricity, airlines and ports. The study concluded that in 11 out of 12 cases studied, divestiture had actually increased national welfare. Welfare gains were especially higher in countries where restructuring and privatization were combined with other policy reforms as part of a major structural change. The study analysed where the changes came from but also impact on the economic agents as winners and losers.[11]

Contrary to expectations, workers and employees were not worse off. Forced retirements or lay-offs affected workers adversely only in the short run. On the other hand, workers did benefit from purchasing at discounted prices the shares of newly privatized enterprises. (This has also been true in countries such as Côte d'Ivoire where the laid-off employees of a beer company obtained priority in allocation of licences for wholesale distribution. In Benin, the laid-off personnel of another beer company later became involved in downstream distribution activities.) Furthermore, employees benefited from employee stock ownership plans (ESOPs) and managers from management buy-outs (MBOs). In some cases, the generous severance payments allowed them to purchase shares in the privatized companies. Some privatization programmes also established a scheme for unemployment benefits as in Chile, and retraining programmes, as in Ghana. In the long run, the workers and employees gained from increased productivity and new investments.

Consumers either remained unaffected or benefited from privatization through increased productivity, improvements in the quality of service as in the case of airlines, telecommunications and electricity, and through more competitive prices.

Some Governments also gained from privatization through the sale price of the enterprises. Mexico collected US$ 15 billion from the sale of 700 enterprises (as of 1992). Also the Governments gained through the reduction of explicit and implicit transfers to these enterprises in the form of investment financing or operational subsidies. They also gained through the expansion of the tax base, as well as new sources of tax revenue.

Private sector indirectly profited from the availability of more reliable and high-quality services to meet the demands in international markets such as timely delivery with more efficient physical and communications infrastructure. Since the sample of companies under review was drawn from non-competitive sectors, the impact on the competitors was necessarily biased and, thus, was not analysed in the study.

Foreign investors reaped the benefits of privatization, whenever the sale price was set low in the beginning and the shares went oversubscribed. This led to the most recent thinking that the Governments would be better off to sell to domestic buyers and to encourage broad-based participation if the price is too low.

Provided they had the time to design well thought out programmes, Governments tried especially hard to increase the welfare gains from privatization. They were determined to create socially acceptable outcomes by trying to improve the benefits from restructuring and privatization among different ethnic and socio-economic groups. The distribution of such benefits depended on how effectively individual Governments and their policy makers utilized the techniques of broad-based public participation during the implementation of privatization programmes. Given the prevailing inequalities of ownership, wealth and income, some Governments more than others perceived privatization as an opportunity to alleviate disparities. Even if the distributional consequences of privatization were not always consistent with the policy makers' original intentions, they were often included in their analysis. These broad-based participation techniques were either one, or a combination, of the following:

- Reservation of controlling shares (even if minority) for core investors – domestic, foreign or joint ventures – who could improve performance and achieve a turnaround;
- Reservation of shares for employees, or give-away schemes;
- Reservation of a certain portion of shares to small investors;
- Deferred public offerings either through Government or through a special agreement with the private enterprise acquiring the shares if it agreed to sell a certain percentage to small investors over time.

None the less, Governments' desire to achieve broad-based ownership conflicted with the financial constraints often encountered in the process. In an attempt to minimize the financial constraints, Governments tried to tap all available domestic capital, attract foreign investment and sell on instalment. At times, lack of available capital became one reason to introduce restructuring without change of ownership.

In countries such as Kenya and Madagascar, private domestic capital was available, but it was concentrated in the hands of the economically dominant ethnic groups. The absence of creative privatization packages, however, increased opposition and retarded the implementation of their programmes. On the other hand, the Government of Malaysia explicitly posted its intention to advance corporate participation of economically disadvantaged ethnic groups through the so-called 'ethnically preferential privatization programme'.

Attracting socially acceptable foreign investment was another keen consideration for many Governments and, at times, became a major obstacle. Some Governments revised their investment codes, and developed a conscious strategy for foreign investment during the privatization process. Anticipating the likely public objections, the Government of Malaysia advocated minority (no more than 25 per cent) foreign investment in privatized entities. Furthermore, it made clear that foreign investment would be directed where: *(a)* foreign expertise was needed and local expertise was not available; *(b)* foreign participation was crucial for export market access and promotion; *(c)* international linkages and exposure were required by the business; *(d)* the supply of domestic capital was not sufficient to absorb all the shares offered.[12]

Selection of Public Enterprises for Restructuring and Privatization

Many developing countries relied on the relevant restructuring and privatization body when selecting enterprises for divestiture. As a first step, the agency in charge reviewed the whole public enterprise portfolio, and determined action for each category of enterprises. The criteria were whether or not the enterprise was running a deficit, had any growth potential, was in the competitive or non-competitive sector, was a monopoly such as a strategic enterprise or a public utility (electricity, telecommunications, port, airline, railways etc.).

It was exactly during this identification and selection phase that many Governments faced the issue of how to restructure the individual enterprise before the prospective sale. A rough cost-benefit analysis for each enterprise was often used as the guiding principle. Both the government bodies in charge of the programme and the individual enterprise managers were to consider a combination of several methods.

Liquidation became a widespread form in all restructuring programmes. It only applied to enterprises when there was no hope of improving the performance of the entity in consideration. If the enterprise was assessed as unviable, there was no other choice but to dispose of it. It was an easier purchase for many local investors. The only problem with liquidations was the inevitable lay-off of total personnel. Both the political opposition and the severance payments imposed political and financial constraints on Governments. The liquidations in several countries, therefore, necessitated the introduction of several retrenchment and retraining programmes for the laid-off workers.

Means of Restructuring Public Enterprises

When enterprises were marked for a fate other than liquidation, Governments followed either the route to restructure for privatization with change of ownership, or they selected the route for restructuring without change of ownership. There were several means available to them: *(a)* legal restructuring; *(b)* competitive restructuring; *(c)* organizational restructuring; *(d)* operational restructuring; *(e)* financial restructuring; *(f)* personnel restructuring; and *(g)* technological restructuring. However, the decision makers had to assess the actual benefits from restructuring and the costs attached to devoting the scarce financial resources and limited technical skills that were domestically available.

Legal restructuring has become essential, particularly in countries like Burkina Faso, Madagascar, Mali and Senegal where severai public enterprises did not have autonomous status at the outset. They were departmental enterprises and their budget was integrated into the budget of their 'tutelle' ministries. They needed to assume corporate identity before they could be transferred to private ownership.

Competitive restructuring often accompanied organizational restructuring. Large conglomerates included the several enterprises not related in production and activity to one another. Therefore, it was essential to dismantle the unrelated activities from one another while breaking down the enterprise into independent competitive segments. The subsequent organizational, operational, personnel and financial restructuring varied from enterprise to enterprise in different countries. In the case of privatizing Mexico's State-owned truck manufacturer Diesel Nacional (DINA), the organizational, financial and personnel restructuring sparked a controversial debate between the prospective buyers and the State as the owner of the enterprise. Before privatization, DINA had been reorganized and minimal personnel restructuring had taken place. However, the Government had no choice but to offer the enterprise for sale with its existing liabilities. Under pressure from DINA's strong automotive labour union, the State insisted that the new buyers accept the enterprise with its existing labour force, with no further labour shedding. Since the Government was very keen on a core investor, the package presented to the potential bidders only allowed them to come up with a counter offer. Their final bids ultimately discounted for the financial and personnel restructuring the Government was not willing to undertake itself.[13]

Technological restructuring was the least desirable option for many Governments. They chose to refrain from technological restructuring or injection of new investment into the enterprise because it had been the least cost effective. It was not always easy for civil servants to judge the future markets effectively. Therefore, such decisions with respect to new investments or technological improvements yielded better results if left to the private sector or to the enterprise's new owners/managers.

Policy makers utilized similar means to restructure the enterprises not selected for privatization. Mostly the strategic or large enterprises that Governments were neither willing nor able to privatize, used all or some of the above-mentioned means of restructuring. Thus, they sought to introduce measures to improve the performance of the enterprises without turning them over to the private sector. The means of restructuring for enterprises not destined for privatization are often summed up in three categories: *(a)* legal restructuring or corporatization; *(b)* commercialization; and *(c)* rehabilitation as detailed below:

- As it was in the case for restructuring for privatization, *legal restructuring* was introduced in order to give the public enterprise a separate legal identity. It was often accompanied with rehabilitation. The new corporate identity freed the public enterprises from tedious procurement procedures, getting credit and foreign exchange on their own terms without prior approval from the Government. Even if the enterprise remained in the Government's portfolio, legal restructuring made it easier to improve enterprise performance and measure it as well.
- *Commercialization* was another method used to reform the public enterprises remaining in the public domain. The Government allowed the public enterprise to perform as a commercial private enterprise by cutting off subsidies, allowing them to set their own prices, and to raise their own investment and working capital. Once commercialized, the public enterprises did not have to comply with the social objectives the Government often insisted upon.
- *Rehabilitation* began with management studies, and led to organizational restructuring. As part of the rehabilitation process, the public enterprises were given new loans from the Government for equipment and for debt restructuring. The Government also

took responsibility for the public enterprises' debt through debt-equity conversion. In some countries, the rehabilitation schemes introduced the performance contracts in an attempt to give the enterprises more autonomy and to hold them accountable only at the end of the contract period.

Modalities of Restructuring and Privatizing Public Enterprises

When the Government evaluated the pros and cons of each means of restructuring, and decided to proceed with the privatization of a particular enterprise, an announcement was floated to the private sector. It indicated the Government's intentions to solicit bids or enquiries of interest. These announcements were mostly prepared by the government agency designated for restructuring and privatization.

All countries followed this overall format, but Malaysia took it a step further. The Government explicitly allowed and even encouraged the private sector (domestic or foreign) to initiate the process. The originality of the scheme was that it included proposals from the private sector to receive government concessions to create new infrastructure facilities such as bridges, expressways, water distribution networks, airports and maritime port terminals. Malaysia became one of the leading countries that invited foreign investors into the build-own-transfer (BOT) or build-own-operate (BOO) schemes to expand and update its infrastructure. Many Latin American countries have recently begun to emulate the Malaysian experiment.[14]

Not all Governments of developing countries were in a position to opt for the change of ownership and proceed with sale privatization. Some tried hard to introduce privatization methods without the change of ownership and opted for non-sale privatization. In some countries, both sale and non-sale privatizations were utilized simultaneously for different enterprises. The most likely candidates for sale privatization became the industrial and commercial enterprises in the competitive sectors. Governments first picked attractive, well-known enterprises for initial sale. These efforts reaped substantial benefits for the privatization agencies in charge as well as for the Governments. Picking the right enterprise helped to generate a better private-sector response and provided a major demonstration effect. The National Commercial Bank in Jamaica, the Turkish Telecommunication Company and the Swarzedz Furniture Company in Poland became examples of selecting winners first. All of these enterprises were over subscribed and had a significant effect rolling further privatizations as well as for stimulating the embryonic stock markets at the time.

The modalities for privatization through change of ownership (or sale privatization) included the following options:

- *Private sale of shares*: In the absence of capital markets, private minority or majority sale to a pre-identified purchaser or a group of buyers was often utilized. Minority sales introduced competition, helped management gain control and prepared the enterprise for a majority sale at a later stage. When Governments needed a competent core investor, they opted for the majority sale to a purchaser. Private majority sales also relied on auctions and let the market decide the sale price through competitive bidding. Several Latin American and all African countries began their privatization programmes with private sale. Mexico started by selling its small and medium-size public enterprises without major restructuring through private majority sales. It gradually moved on to more complicated transactions.

- *Sale of government or enterprise assets*: Governments had to downsize the enterprise and to sell its assets separately along its distinct lines of activities. In some cases, the public enterprise itself disposed of its assets while restructuring. This method made the enterprise more saleable to the private sector.

- *Public offering of equity*: Governments utilized this method by offering the public blocks of stock it held in wholly or partially owned public enterprises. As mentioned earlier, public offerings required well-functioning capital markets. Governments, furthermore, utilized this method to create a stock market while simultaneously achieving widespread ownership. However, the latter was only achieved as long as Governments introduced public awareness campaigns and educated the general public on how they could participate, and what they were to gain (or lose) from it.

- *Management buy-outs* (MBOs): The acquisition by a small group of managers of a controlling stake in a newly privatized enterprise constituted an MBO. Chile and Côte d'Ivoire are among the countries that widely utilized these methods.

- *Employee stock-ownership plan* (ESOPs): This modality allowed the employees to acquire blocks of shares in the newly privatized enterprises. It also led to widespread distribution of ownership among the population. As long as the ESOPs remained only a minority, there was no need to fear sacrificing efficiency in exchange for attaining better equity. Chile again utilized this method extensively.

- *Injection of new capital* to the enterprise through joint ventures: In some cases Governments decided to dilute their equity position by allowing new capital in a public enterprise. The purpose was mostly rehabilitation or expansion. The resulting joint ventures endowed the enterprise not only with new capital, but also with new technology and management skills. Furthermore, they helped improve the investment climate in the country for other foreign and domestic investors. However, Governments could not readily find joint-venture partners. Latin American and Asian countries managed to attract foreign joint-venture partners more successfully than African countries.

- *Debt-equity swaps*: The international debt holders wishing to buy the enterprise swapped the country's international commercial bank debt worth a fraction of its face value in secondary markets, and became equity owners in the newly privatized enterprises. Swaps were widely used, especially in Argentina's and Chile's privatization schemes through which both countries attracted flight capital. These debt-equity swaps helped to reduce the financial constraint as well as to improve the investment climate in the country. However, Governments received only a fraction of the face value of their international debt through the debt-equity swaps. This led to a controversy on the overall welfare gains and losses for the society through these swaps. The opponents of the debt-equity swaps argue that the Governments could have been made better off by selling the public enterprise first, and repaying or repurchasing international debt in secondary markets. The proponents, on the other hand, believe that the swaps not only helped speed up the privatization process, but also eased the foreign exchange constraint for paying back the international debt.

- *Combination of all the above methods*: Most successful programmes made use of all the above modalities, and combined them creatively in a variety of ways to achieve the outcome they had envisioned in the beginning of the privatization process.

Both efficiency and equity considerations forced the Governments to utilize all these modalities for the most effective and desirable outcome.

The modalities for privatization without change of ownership (or non-sale privatization) were often referred to as privatization of management, or reforming the enterprise along commercial lines. They included the following variety of options:

- *Service contracts*: These contracts were utilized by the public enterprises in the infrastructure sector. They were designed to transfer to private suppliers the responsibility for either delivering a specific service at lower costs, or providing expertise that is lacking in the public enterprise or too expensive to maintain in public payrolls. Pakistan's railways have been contracting out catering, cleaning and ticketing. Chile's public water company has transferred meter reading and fee collections to private contractors. The same company has been known to have encouraged its own staff to leave and compete for such service contracts.[15]
- *Management contracts*: These contracts were extensively utilized in hotels and airlines as well as in some industrial enterprises and infrastructure services in Africa and Asia. They were designed for a private company, foreign or domestic, that agreed to manage the public enterprise for a fee. These fee-for-service arrangements included a broad scope of operations and maintenance, usually for a period of three to five years. The new managers did not assume any commercial risk or responsibility with respect to investments or capital expenditures. In some cases, the fee for the management contract was paid by international aid agencies. In 1989, the National Electricity and Water Utility in Guinea-Bissau was near bankruptcy, and it entered into a two-year management contract with the National Electricity Company of France, another public enterprise. According to the terms of the contract, the French enterprise took over the operation of the utility in Guinea-Bissau, and the compensation was partly paid on fixed fees by the French Ministry of Cooperation, and partly on a share of the revenue-based profits of the utility.[16]
- *Lease contracts*: In contrast to management contracts, the leasing arrangement required that the private company, foreign and

domestic, assumes the commercial risk in operating and maintaining the enterprise, in addition to a pre-set fee for use of assets. But the lessee had no responsibility for capital expenditure and investments while the public owner (lessor) remained responsible for fixed investments and debt servicing. The lease contractor usually collected the revenue directly, and returned an agreed portion to the public authority as rental or licence fee. The duration of the contract was often between 6 and 10 years. This has been used in African industrial sectors (steel and oil refinery in Togo) and public utilities (electricity in Côte d'Ivoire) where Governments could not attract foreign investors.[17]

The latter case illustrates an example from the infrastructure sector. The deterioration of the performance of the public enterprise in charge of the power sector in Côte d'Ivoire led to a major restructuring in 1990 whereby operations and maintenance functions for generation, transmission and distribution were transferred under a leasing arrangement to a new joint venture, the Electricity Company of Côte d'Ivoire. This company was owned 51 per cent by a consortium of two French companies, and 49 per cent by domestic investors. While the public enterprise responsible for the power sector continued to own the facilities and bore responsibility for investments, sector policy and planning, the new joint-venture company became in charge of operations and maintenance. This leasing arrangement proved extremely successful as the duration of the power outages was reduced, business operations were computerized and operating subsidies were eliminated.[18]

- *Concessions*: A concession contract incorporated all the features of a leasing arrangement, but gave the contractor an additional responsibility for financing certain specified extensions or replacement of fixed assets. Such arrangements ranged from power, water supply and treatment, solid waste disposal and treatment, ports, railways, urban metro systems, toll roads and telecommunications. In these arrangements, the investment plan proposed by the contractor was reviewed by the authority issuing the contract. Concessions often last 15–30 years, depending on the life of the investments, and they are often renewed. The concession of water supply services in Côte d'Ivoire for a 20-year contract, and the concession arrangements in water supply, sewage and railways in Argentina are among the few successful examples.[19]

- *BOT/BOO schemes*: There are few examples of successfully negotiated BOT schemes in developing countries. These private arrangements are gaining new importance where Governments can no longer borrow sufficient investment directly and finance their own investments. The privately financed BOT or BOO schemes are used to build the essential infrastructure projects where Governments failed to have the necessary financial resources. These schemes indirectly demonstrated Governments' willingness to rely on foreign capital to make its infrastructure and industrial sector competitive. Malaysia was the leader in setting up these schemes, and more recently, several Asian and Latin American countries have begun to emulate the Malaysian experience in expanding their infrastructure sector.

- *Performance contracts*: In contrast to all the above arrangements with the private sector, the performance contracts relied on the existing public enterprise managers and expected them to act as 'private managers' without handing the enterprise over to the private sector. Many developing countries have increasingly begun to utilize performance contracts to restructure their strategic public enterprises and sometimes to complement their efforts to privatize their commercial and industrial enterprises, as is the case in Ghana and Nigeria.

Compared to management contracts and leasing, performance contracts had a much longer history. They were first introduced to the developing countries by the French in the early 1980s. The French-style performance contracts (originated in France as 'contrat de plan' in 1967), became popular in countries such as Benin, Bolivia, Morocco, Senegal and Tunisia. Later on, an improved version of French performance contracts, the signalling system, emerged and gained recognition in several countries such as Bangladesh, Ghana, Pakistan, Republic of Korea and Venezuela. The Government of India experimented with both systems. Until 1988, it utilized the French-style performance contracts and switched thereafter to the signalling system.

In essence, performance contracts were performance agreements between the Government and the public enterprises. Their common purpose was to reconcile the conflicting objectives of public enterprises, to clarify their relationship with Government and to facilitate performance evaluation based on results rather than on conformity with bureaucratic rules and regulations. These contracts included both quantitative and qualitative performance targets against which the actual performance could be measured.

In contrast to the French-style performance contracts, the signalling system spelled out a *performance evaluation system*, a *performance information system* and a *performance incentive system*. The performance evaluation system specified the socially desirable performance; the performance information system helped to accurately measure economic performance; and the performance incentive system rewarded managers and staff on the basis of actual, versus targeted, performance.

Performance contracts led to performance improvement in many public enterprises in several countries. Most recently, eastern European countries such as Hungary and Romania have begun to introduce performance contracts to their public enterprises with the assistance of the World Bank. Some developing countries, on the other hand, had mixed results with their performance contract experience. As was the case with privatization, performance contracts only worked as long as there existed a high level of political commitment among various levels of Government, academic and research institutions, and at the enterprise level. Their success was correlated with the level of training and skills of the key officials in Government, in the monitoring agency as well as within the public enterprise. All these actors were responsible to monitor, implement and evaluate the performance contracts. As in the case of Senegal, the agency in charge of the public enterprise reform (la Délégation pour la Réforme du Secteur Parapublic) did not establish a coordination between the Government and the enterprises with performance contracts. More importantly, Senegalese performance contracts were far away from the signalling system and did not include a performance information and a performance incentive system.[20]

Conclusion

A large number of developing countries are today at various stages of planning or implementing restructuring and privatization programmes.

Successful restructuring and privatization programmes worked best in a competitive economic environment with an expanding private sector. They were primarily monitored and implemented by dedicated institutions with full authority. These institutions carefully planned the restructuring and privatization programmes and clearly defined their objectives. These objectives were subsequently communicated to the wider public through the media. This, in turn, demonstrated Governments' political commitment, and helped to establish from the start the necessary political and social consensus.

Despite their overwhelming success, restructuring and privatization programmes were both difficult and costly. Governments had to fight off the inherent political opposition from the political parties, labour unions, public enterprise managers, private sector competitors and the general public. At the same time, Governments had to balance carefully both the efficiency and equity objectives. The utilization of broad-based participation techniques gave them the much-needed political support at the outset, and created a more equitable distribution of ownership among different ethnic and socio-economic groups. However, newly privatized enterprises could only work efficiently and create investment and employment as long as the new owners were fully capable of restructuring and operating them after the privatization transaction itself.

Yet privatization was not the only, and certainly not the most popular, prescription for enterprise restructuring. Thousands of public enterprises remain (and will remain) under government ownership without prospect of being transferred to the private sector. These enterprises have been looking out for alternative solutions. A great many of them have already opted to privatize their management without change of ownership. Service contracts, management contracts, leasing, concessions and, most importantly, performance contracts have begun to play a crucial role in improving performance of these enterprises. At the same time, the methodologies to evaluate and to reward managers for performance have become increasingly sophisticated.

The real challenge for many Governments continues to be how to design and implement the right mix of restructuring and privatization programmes. The ministries and governmental agencies entrusted with this task could learn from the success stories in other developing countries. However, policy makers need to carefully assess the inherent political and financial obstacles in their own countries to be able to launch the most effective programmes with the most desirable and acceptable outcome – socially, politically and economically.

Notes

1. This paper focuses on the restructuring and privatization experience of the developing countries in Latin America, Asia and Africa, and excludes the eastern and central European experience which was more specifically addressed in the previous chapter.
2. Revealed compared advantage (RCA) is the most common export performance indicator. RCA = $(x/X) / (x_w/X_w)$, where x is the value of the exported product from a particular country and X is the value of total exports from that country, x_w is the value of the world's exports in that product and X_w is the value of total world exports. RCA values vary between 0 and infinity. Values above unity indicate the comparative advantage of a particular country in that particular product while values below unity suggest a comparative disadvantage.
3. Gökgür (1993).
4. Lieberman (1993), p. 12.
5. Gökgür (1994).
6. Lieberman (1993), p. 12.
7. Gökgür, Krakoff and Gianni (1993).
8. Leeds (1989), pp. 741–46.
9. Gökgür (1989).
10. Under the leadership of Professor Leroy Jones.
11. Galal and Shirley (eds) (1994).
12. Jomo (1993), p. 442.
13. Gökgür (1989).
14. Hensley and White (1993), p. 79.
15. Estache (1994), p. 24.
16. Kessides (1993), p. 30.
17. Shirley and Kikeri (1993), p. 26.
18. Kessides (1993), p. 32.
19. Ibid. p. 33.
20. Gökgür (1990).

References

Estache, Antonio (1994), 'Making Public Infrastructure Entities Commercial', in *Finance and Development*, the IMF and the World Bank, September, pp. 22–25.

Galal, Ahmed and Mary Shirley (eds) (1994), 'Does Privatization Deliver?', Highlights from a World Bank conference, Economic Institute of the World Bank.

Gökgür, Nilgün (1989), 'Privatization of Diesel Nacional (DINA) of Mexico', Teaching Case, Public Enterprise Workshop, Harvard Institute for International Development.

____ (1990), 'A New Performance Contract for the Senegalese Electricity Company (SENELEC)', Teaching Case, Public Enterprise Workshop, Harvard Institute for International Development.

____ (1993), 'Export Profiles, World Market Shares, and Revealed Comparative Advantage: Asia vs. Latin America', Synthesis of Comparative Research for the course on Management in Developing Countries, Harvard Business School.

____ (1994), 'Emerging Markets: The Rising Role of Portfolio Investment Flows to Developing Countries', *Working Paper No. 94–053*, Harvard Business School.

Gökgür, N., C. Krakoff and P. Gianni (1993), 'Madagascar: Privatization Assessment', Report submitted to USAID/Madagascar on behalf of Abt Associates, Inc. and Price Waterhouse, Inc.

Hensley, Matthew L. and Edward P. White (1993), 'The Privatization Experience in Malaysia', *Colombia Journal of World Business*, Spring.

Jomo, K. S. (1993), 'Privatization in Malaysia', in Thomas Clarke and Christos Pitelis (eds), *Political Economy of Privatization*.

Kessides, Christine (1993), 'Institutional Options for the Provision of Infrastructure', *World Bank Discussion Paper No. 212*, World Bank.

Leeds, Roger (1989), 'Malaysia: Genesis of a Privatization Transaction', *World Development*, vol. 17, No. 5.

Lieberman, Ira W. (1993), 'Privatization: The Theme of the 1990s', *Colombia Journal of World Business*, Spring.

Shirley, Mary and Sunita Kikeri (1993), 'Privatization: The Lessons of Experience', Country Economics Department, World Bank.

4. Institutional Support to Restructuring: the Treuhandanstalt in Germany

*Christa Luft**

The Pre-1989 Era

From 1949 to 1989 the former German Democratic Republic (GDR) followed the model of a centrally planned economy. Its main characteristics were:

* Dominating State-owned property (see Table 4.1);
* Large vertically integrated conglomerates – called combines – which tended to be highly autarchic in their trading patterns;
* Planning from the top;
* State-controlled price formation;
* Non-convertible ·currency;
* State monopoly over foreign trade;
* Integration of the national economy into COMECON.

The Fall of the Berlin Wall

After the sudden collapse of the Berlin Wall on 9 November 1989, a new Government headed by Hans Modrow was sworn in. It consisted in its first form of representatives of 5 (later 13) political parties and movements.

The Modrow Government aimed at:

* Normalizing the political and economic relations with the Federal Republic of Germany (FRG), and establishing in a first phase

*Berlin Institut für Internationale Bildung.

78

a community of interests based on the exchange of contracts while moving towards a confederation of both German States;
- Initiating a home-grown transition process to a market economy, based on a variety of property forms, a competitive private sector, and a supportive industrial policy framework.

Table 4.1 *Share of different property forms in the industrial output of the former GDR (in per cent, at current prices)*

Year	State-owned	Cooperative	Private
1950	49.2	6.1	44.7
1960	68.0	15.2	16.8
1970	68.8	16.2	15.0
1980	86.2	9.8	4.0
1985	85.5	10.4	4.1
1988		95.7	4.3
1989		95.7	4.3

Source: Statistical Yearbook of the GDR, Berlin 1990, p. 105.

In order to stimulate private business and competition, the Modrow Government:

- Introduced freedom of trade;
- Created the legal basis for setting up joint ventures;
- Allowed the denationalization of former privately owned small and medium-sized companies, which had been nationalized in 1972;
- Began to convert the vast State-owned holding enterprises (combines) into capital companies, and established on 1 March 1990 the Treuhandanstalt as a major shareholder.

The Treuhandanstalt acquired control over most of GDR's corporate assets although it saw itself more as an instrument of industrial policy. The original mandate of the Treuhandanstalt did not aim at the rapid privatization of State-owned property. The institution took over the trusteeship of the State-owned property in the interest of the people of the GDR.

From the Fall of the Berlin Wall to Reunification

At the beginning of February 1990, the coalition Government of the Federal Republic of Germany (FRG), headed by Chancellor Kohl, offered the GDR Government an economic and monetary union. Soon afterwards, on 18 March of the same year, a democratic election took place; it was won by Kohl's Christian Democrats who, together with their coalition partners, had campaigned for the swiftest possible route to market economy and unity.

On 18 May 1990 a treaty spelling out the details of an economic and currency union was agreed upon between the GDR and FRG Governments. The treaty, which took effect on 1 July, introduced a unified economic space across the whole of Germany, abolished tariff restrictions, introduced FRG economic laws and instituted the deutsche mark (DM) as the official currency for both. Considering that the effective exchange rate at that time was about one deutsche mark to four marks (M), the exchange rate was set at a generous DM 1 for M 1 for most money in circulation and DM 1 for M 2 for some savings and corporate debt. By this time it was also clear that a full political union would not be far behind. On 3 October 1990, the German reunification was formally complete.

The Post-Unification Period: a New Mandate for the Treuhandanstalt

Owing to the forthcoming prospect of a currency union and the increased momentum towards full reunification, privatization became a priority, and the new GDR Government, headed by Lothar de Maiziere, amended accordingly the mandate of the Treuhandanstalt. On 17 June 1990, a trusteeship was passed by the Government, which transferred all State-owned enterprises and property to the Treuhandanstalt and further stipulated that, by the date of a complete economic and currency union (that is, 1 July 1990), all enterprises should be automatically converted into FRG-style corporations (either as limited liability companies (GmbHs) or in the form of stock companies (AGs)).

The new Treuhandanstalt became an independent entity constituted under public law. From the date of the economic union, it has been reporting directly to the Ministry of Finance at Bonn.

Since June 1990 its objectives have been:

- To privatize – mostly through 100 per cent sales;
- To restructure (with a view to privatizing at a later stage);
- To close the companies under its control, when warranted.

In addition, the Treuhandanstalt had been entrusted with the task of dismantling the larger combines, so that the original 8,000 industrial companies later turned into about 12,300 smaller enterprises.

The Privatization Experience

Privatization in the former GDR began rather hesitantly. This was due to the fact that the political union was not fully complete; the ownership problem had not been resolved, and because former GDR companies had lost, immediately after the currency union, much of their domestic market to superior goods from the FRG. Furthermore, traditional trade patterns with former COMECON countries had been severely disrupted, as barter-type exchanges had given way to hard cash settlements – at a considerably slower pace due to critical shortages of convertible currency.

Treuhandanstalt executives were initially compelled to keep the shell-shocked former GDR companies afloat. A total of DM 20 billion in liquidity credit was handed out in the first three months after the currency union, merely to ensure that the companies could meet their wage bill.

Despite these obstacles, by the end of 1990 the Treuhandanstalt had established a lasting structure based around eight central departments, each one responsible for a particular industrial sector together with a general function. Department One, for instance, was delegated responsibility for the machine-building sector, while assuming at the same time overall responsibility for the privatization policy.

Not only the headquarters, but also the 15 regional offices of the Treuhandanstalt underwent a similar restructuring. Experienced managers from the FRG were hired to run the regional offices, and they were given direct responsibility for all companies under their purview, employing fewer than 1,500 people (about two thirds of the total 8,000).

Enterprise privatizations, which numbered only a few hundred cases by the end of 1990, soared at the beginning of 1991. Building on the strong impetus of the legislation ('Treuhandgesetz') of 17 June 1990, the Treuhandanstalt released in October 1990 a Business Policy Guide, clearly stating its priority to privatize, rather than to restructure, companies or parts of companies – in the firm conviction that privatization was the best way to restructure an enterprise.

The Treuhandanstalt was none the less prepared to initiate and support restructuring programmes in non-privatized enterprises, provided the management was able to present a convincing recovery plan to restore the firm's competitiveness within a reasonable time frame.

The agency's privatization policy was shaped by its commitment to transfer companies into the private sector as quickly as possible after careful evaluation, while at the same time endeavouring to attract a large number of bidders in order to gain a realistic assessment of a company's worth.

When making enquiries about companies before submitting tenders, potential buyers were instructed to take into consideration the Treuhandanstalt's particular requirements. Indeed, in addition to the bidding price, the offer was expected to contain detailed information on:

- The retention of jobs, and future employment policy in general;
- The continued operation and modernization of the company by the purchaser and the investment required to that end;
- The implications for the suppliers and subcontractors in the new federal States.

The Achievements

Three years after the second Treuhandanstalt came into being, its achievements can be broadly assessed as follows:

- By the end of 1994 all of the former SOEs will have been transferred to new owners – with the exception of about 100 companies (see Table 4.2).
- About 80 per cent of all privatized companies are sold to buyers of the FRG, nearly 6 per cent to foreigners and approximately

14 per cent to managers of the former GDR or to the staff of the respective companies.

* The new owners have given contractual assurances regarding 1.5 million jobs and private investment figures totalling over DM 190 billion. Not all of these promises were fulfilled within the prescribed delays.
* The proceeds from the sale of State assets amount to nearly DM 49 billion.
* From 1990 until mid-1994, the former GDR lost more than one third of its total working places and nearly half of the industrial jobs. The official rate of unemployment stands at 16 per cent. If one includes, however, the people in early retirement, the participants in retraining courses and the commuters who found jobs in the western part of Germany, the unemployment rate rises to approximately 35 per cent.
* On 31 December 1994, the Treuhandanstalt was officially dissolved, as clearly stipulated from the outset in its statutes.

Table 4.2   Achievements of the Treuhandanstalt (Number of enterprises)

	31 December 1993	31 January 1994	28 February 1994	30 March 1994
Portfolio	12,246	12,267	12,272	12,306
Reduction by:				
• Privatization				
– Fully privatized	5,833	5,914	5,944	6,020
– More than 50 per cent privatized	347	331	328	309
• Denationalization	1,658	1,660	1,647	1,649
• Transfer to the towns and districts	261	260	262	264
• Liquidation				
– Completed	78	85	92	92
– Ongoing	3,118	3,134	3,152	3,184
Remainder	951	883	847	788

Source: Treuhandanstalt.

Conclusions

The transition from a centrally planned to a market economy calls first of all for creating a competitive environment which should not be equated, somewhat simplistically, to the full-blown privatization of public property.

Second, the speed of privatization must be adjusted to the prevailing potential for job creation, and training programmes must be designed to alleviate the disastrous effect of a massive and sudden contraction of employment.

Finally, the speed of privatization must also be tailored to the prospects for attracting internal and external private capital, as well as entrepreneurial talents in order to modernize product lines and create competitive markets.

5. Economic Reforms, Industrial Restructuring and Multi-agent Decision-making

*Philippe R. Scholtès**

General Background

Since the 1980s, a growing number of developing countries have turned to a market economy as a way of accelerating the pace of their economic development through a more rational allocation of resources. Towards the end of the decade, this trend was dramatically quickened with the rise of the iron curtain and the dissolution of the former USSR.

The underlying motivation was that the centralized planning approach, in which the government sector predominated, had fallen short of its objectives on both growth and equity grounds. On the contrary, it had created deep internal and external imbalances and a poorly performing and structurally inadequate industrial network in the manufacturing sector.

In a great many cases, the State had overstepped its role of providing public services and had become increasingly involved in a broad range of production activities, often with unsatisfactory results.

This unsustainable situation had often sent economies into a vicious circle marked by an excessive concentration of national resources in the public sector, faulty management of industrial enterprises and the poor performance that this entails, a general lack of competitiveness, reliance on trade barriers and price controls to protect the domestic market and, finally, severe structural distortions.

*United Nations Industrial Development Organization, Vienna.

In the wake of the 1980s, far-reaching reforms were instituted, especially in the developing countries and in eastern Europe, with a view to curbing this disastrous spiral and resuming growth on firmer premises. The private sector was given a leading role in manufacturing activities, while the State was confined to the role of supporter and, where necessary, arbiter in the free play of market forces.

The instruments used in this reform process include a complete overhaul of the production apparatus and privatization efforts aimed, in the short term, at alleviating public debt and, in the longer term, at fully fledged industrial restructuring.

Formulation of Industrial Strategies

In a market economy, success in any industrial endeavour is closely linked to the capacity to gain or to maintain a competitive position on domestic or international markets. This, in turn, calls for the coordination of a number of initiatives to be taken by the industrial enterprise, the industrial environment and the State.

An enabling environment in this context calls for the concurrence of a series of factors aggregated, for the sake of clarity, in four levels:

- At the level of the *policy set-up*:

  - A macroeconomic and legal framework conducive to private initiatives, including an overall framework for privatization, and particularly, clear-cut laws on property rights;
  - Appropriate industrial, trade, taxation and investment policies;
  - Transparent administrative and regulatory procedures;
  - Above all, economic and political stability to encourage long-term capital formation.

- At the level of the *business environment*:

  - Supportive industry-related services that nurture entrepreneurship and encourage new ventures in the manufacturing sector;
  - Adequate infrastructures, be they physical (roads, telecommunications, utilities), institutional (industry associations, chambers of commerce, industrial parks and export process-

ing zones), financial (an industry-friendly banking sector and organized capital markets, possibly with a special window for new entries in the small-scale sector).

- At the level of the *firm's production function*:

  - Efficient technological processes, which in turn calls for adequate mechanisms for technology transfers and attractive schemes to bolster inflows of foreign direct investment;
  - Qualified skills and appropriate human resource development programmes;
  - Sound management practices, marketing networks, etc.

- At the level of *industrial organization*:

  As experience shows, an essential factor of private sector development lies with the quality and density of the linkages across industrial enterprises and related services. The reliance on market mechanisms to allocate resources translates, as far as manufacturing is concerned, into a continuous quest to achieve, sustain or strengthen a competitive stronghold. At the same time, the complexity of today's manufacturing processes compounded by various market failures, calls for increasingly sophisticated business relationships within clusters of manufacturing enterprises and industry-related services. Competitiveness issues, as well as private sector development altogether, must be addressed in this particular context.

Although they by no means represent an exhaustive list, the factors outlined above highlight the complexity of the manufacturing activity and of its growth process. Strengthening a competitive position, and hence a strong and sustained growth path, depends on how insightful are the decisions taken, both by individual enterprises in their business plans and by the State in its socio-economic programmes.

Strategic choices are often made by the two sides independently; thus, improved competitiveness ultimately derives from a complex decision-making process that involves a large number of economic agents in a context of uncertainty, as these initiatives are typically forward looking.

From the Market Paradigm to the Real Economy

Market signals, and especially the resulting price structure, are theoretically the best guides to an efficient distribution of resources. Yet the theory presupposes a number of conditions that are rarely verifiable in practice owing to a variety of real-life contingencies such as trade constraints, restrictive policies, disparities in the influence of economic agents, product differentiation and uneven flows of information.

These market failures alter the economic equation and generate undesirable responses, such as a growing informal sector where firms benefit from unwarranted tax holidays, attempts by enterprises to deflect competition by seeking market dominance through oligopolistic positions or collusive agreements, fraudulent imports, etc. These market deficiencies call for the State to play a new role, that of arbiter of the free and fair play of market forces.

Yet the State's support to fostering development in a market economy also encompasses proactive economic policies, particularly in the industrial field, designed to support the expansion and accumulation of technological capabilities. In that case, the increased sophistication of manufacturing today brings together, in a complex decision-making process, a group of private and public economic agents guided by specific, not necessarily converging, objectives.

All decision-making processes comprise an initial situation (or 'state' in decision theory), a target (or 'consequence', deemed desirable in the light of certain criteria) and a strategy (or 'act') for moving from one to the other. The planning process consists of mapping out the most appropriate scenario to drive the economy or the sector from the present to the desired situation, given the prevailing constraints. In a command economy, the planning process translated into a centralized allocation of available resources to productive activities aimed at quantitative output targets. An industrial plan in this context typically featured a stocktaking of physical resources, demand forecasts and a public investment programme to lay out the required capacities to service future needs. Responsibility for the implementation of the plan rested exclusively with the centre or the public authority.[1]

A market economy on the contrary displays a multitude of agents, firms and consumers that interact on a daily basis and eventually shape the economy. They pursue specific agendas, responding to decentralized market signals and distribute resources accordingly. The process of strategic planning is therefore fundamentally different, and probably far more complex, in that it must apprehend the economic rationale underlying production and consumption patterns, and discern areas where market forces alone may fail to deliver long-term growth and sustainable social development.

The planner, i.e. the Government, becomes in this context but one player among others in the decision-making process that drives the industrialization of the country. Indeed, in the early 1980s, policy formulation became an issue of optimal control under uncertainty. Recent developments in game theory during the 1980s further expanded the model to incorporate the idea of non-cooperative games between the State and private economy, where both sides pursue specific agendas and move either simultaneously (Nash) or in a leader-follower sequence (Stackelberg). The latter models have witnessed extensive research in such fields as 'tâtonnement' processes to portray converging mechanisms, persisting disequilibria, incentive-compatibility and reputational equilibria associated with payoffs and penalties. Non-cooperative games are often of a zero-sum type, which means that the gains of some are the losses of others, and the outcome is not Pareto efficient.

Uncertainty and Cooperative Games: an Axiomatic Analysis

Any industrializing economy typically features two or three classes of agents; the essence of the transition process precisely lies with the gradual transfer of State-owned enterprises to an emerging class of private employers (see Figure 5.1). An industrialization strategy, as well as the future course of action in any other sector of economic activity, is seen in this context as the outcome of a game between these three classes of players.

While the respective objectives of labour and employers are clear enough and well documented, it is arguably a fact of political life in any democracy that elected Governments primarily react to stimuli such as popularity and re-election prospects, which overriding concerns in turn shape their socio-economic policies.

Assuming that voters' expectations are relatively invariant across countries at comparable stages of development, the very alternance at the helm of western Governments[2] of democrats, labour or socialists on the one hand, and republicans, conservatives or liberals on the other, underscores the absence of a clear-cut economic growth scenario that would *a priori* satisfy the electorate.[3] A likely explanation can be found in the varying wavelength between political cycles (that is, the time between two consecutive elections) and business cycles, or the natural sequence of peaks and troughs inherent in any economic activity.

Figure 5.1   Changing patterns of industrial organization in transition economies

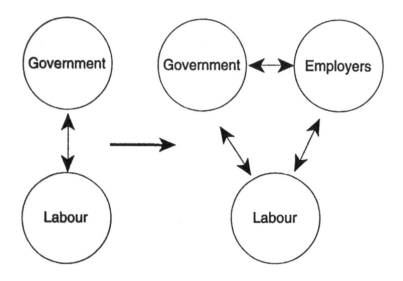

The likelihod of a natural convergence[4] across the distinct objectives of these three classes of agents appears rather remote, except perhaps when the level of industrial organization is so low at the outset that the mere fact of improving the exchange of information between Government and industry yields positive payoffs to the large majority of those concerned.

In the case of industrial development strategies, the decision-making process brings in a range of economic agents that often do not agree on the nature of the initial and the target situation, and who will inevitably disagree on the steps to be taken to move between the two.

The uncertainty implicit in this relationship ultimately causes heavy economic and social losses at precisely the time when a rational management of the transition process requires just the opposite: the mobilization of all national resources towards achieving common goals and a consensus on a practicable and realistic *modus operandi* to that end.

Uncertainty prevails at several levels: the grasp of the initial situation due to exogenous and unpredictable effects, the assessment of the consequences (see Drèze, 1987 on state-dependent utility, adaptive utility and subjective probability), restrictions on the sets of feasibles acts, model specification and parameters of the mapping between states and consequences. At times it is additive (homogeneous of degree one), but it can also be multiplicative, and therefore seriously undermine the effectiveness of the decision-making process, as illustrated here in a general equilibrium setting.

- *The deterministic model: the Arrow–Debreu economy*

Consider a finite economy with n firms j and l commodities h. In a Euclidean space R^l (fitted with the necessary vectorial and topological properties), any firm j may be depicted by its production set Y_j, which represents all technically feasible combinations of inputs and outputs. Let $Y = \Sigma_j \ Y_j$ be the total production set of the economy, with of course $Y \subset R^l$.

Assume in this first section, that no singularity occurs. In particular, Y is convex and so is Y_j for all j, there are no production externalities and the State is a producer among others.

*Figure 5.2   An agent's strategy
in a deterministic
environment*

*Figure 5.3   The stochastic
scenario*

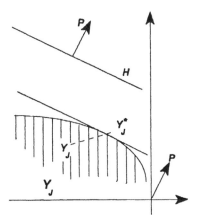
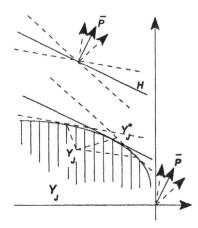

- At any time, the situation of the j–th firm may be identified by a point $y_j = (+y_j, -y_j)$ in R^l, where the $+y_j$ component (resp. $-y_j$) accounts for j's outputs (resp. inputs) at y_j. Note that in a real world, and especially in developing economies, y_j is likely to be an interior point of Y_j.

  Let p be the l–vector of prices prevailing in our economy. p is taken as given by all producers j, as under the standard assumption of the theory, none of them has the bargaining power to influence the market prices. p measures then the economic value of all goods and services, inputs and outputs alike. Moreover, since in an Arrow–Debreu economy, commodities are dated and located, p carries also information on interest rates and exchange rates.

  Given the posted price vector p and the supply y_j, their inner product $p.y_j = \Pi_j$ is a scalar measuring the difference between j's sales (or market value of outputs) and its costs (or market value of inputs). Thus Π_j measures the net value of j's activity, or j's profit.

  Furthermore, the theory assumes that the firm's behaviour is steered by an objective of profit maximization under the constraint of a given technology. In other words, the j–th firm will seek a production pattern y_j^* such that $p.y_j^* \geqslant p.y_j$ for all $y_j \in Y_j$, and $y_j^* \in Y_j$. Define then in R^l a class of hyperplanes H, with $H = \{z, z' \in R^l \mid p.(z-z') = 0\}$. p is clearly normal to H, in fact $p = \nabla H$.

  By Minkowski's theorem of separating hyperplanes, the optimal production pattern of j is y_j^*, with $y_j^* \in H$ and $y_j^* \in \bar{Y}_j$ the closure of Y_j in R^l. It is therefore profit improving for the firm j to move from y_j to y_j^*, and the vector $(y_j^*-y_j)$ indicates the shortest route to do so (see Figure 5.2).

  In the jargon of business management, the assessment of $p,$[5] Y_j (especially $\bar{Y}_j$, a certainly non-trivial exercise in developing countries) and y_j is called strategic analysis. The vector $(y_j^*-y_j)$ is referred to as strategic choice, whereas strategic implementation accounts for the actual route to be taken, which is not necessarily the shortest one in R^l.

- *Stochastic departures*

  Suppose now that the producer j has only a blurred vision of the actual price system $p.$[6] To formalize this, consider that to p is attached a certain variance σ_j, p becomes a random variable with a specific multivariate distribution of probability around its mathematical expectation $E(p)$.

To producer j, the price system will then no longer appear as a vector, but rather as a (convex) cone in R^l. Likewise, H will appear fuzzy to j: the result of j's maximization programme, despite our convexity assuption on Y_j, is no longer a unique y_j^*, but becomes a compact subset $\overline{Y}_j^* \subset \overline{Y}_j$, provided $\overline{Y}_j$ is C^2-smooth over a suitable neighbourhood of y_j^*.

Similarly, the mathematical representation of j's strategy is no longer a vector, but a cone with vertex y_j. The supply function $y_j^*(p)$ becomes then a supply correspondence mapping the price cone P onto Y_j^*.

This situation is likely to bring the individual producer j to an infra-optimal situation, characterized by a non-efficient use of resources at given prices. The outcome is worse even at aggregate level, when the very notion of a general equilibrium is jeopardized (see Figure 5.3).

- *Aggregation, clusters and subsystems*

The aggregation of the production sets of the n producers j yields a total production set $Y = \Sigma_j \ Y_j$.

It was assumed earlier in this chapter that at an individual level, none of the producers had the power to influence the prices (i.e. the producers were strictly price-takers). However, it is clear that at aggregate level, the total supply y^* will both depend on and influence the prices. In other words, $y^* = f(p)$ and $p = f(y^*)$. So far, this section has concentrated on the supply side of the market. One may reach similar conclusions looking now at the demand side, with an aggregate demand $x^* = f(p)$ and $p = f(x^*)$. The central result of general equilibrium theory lies with the existence proof of a fixed point breaking that circularity and matching producers' with consumers' plans. The powerful virtue of that argument is that, although p is determined at aggregate level, the same price system, taken this time as given by the n individual producers j (respectively the m individual consumers i) will yield n individual optima y_j^* (resp. m optima x_i^*) such that $y^* = \Sigma_j \ y_j^*$ (resp. $x^* = \Sigma_i \ x_i^*$).

This is the standard result in an Arrow–Debreu economy. However, if a deterministic price-system p is replaced by a random variable, the argument collapses, as different agents with incomplete information are likely to refer to different prices to guide their choices.

The outcome of the process is not an economic equilibrium, in so far as it does not result from an optimization programme and therefore does not display any of the equity and efficiency features associated to Walrasian equilibria. Instead, the emerging situation depicts an inefficient allocation of resources marked on the supply side by low degrees of capacity and labour utilization and, generally speaking, a sub-optimal use of inputs, yielding low productivity, competitiveness and profitability.

Improving the situation towards a general equilibrium goes through reducing the variance σ_j the j-th agent attaches to the price system. The question is, how to disseminate upgraded information through the set of producers. Notice that for any j, Y_j is actually a subspace of R^l, with a lower dimension. Note moreover that the lack of interlinkages in the productive sector is a typical feature of developing economies. Therefore if Y is the total production set of such a country, Y is not dense in R^l, but appears rather as the union of possibly disconnected Y_js.

Some of those individual production sets share common dimension(s) and are grouped therefore in clusters of production sets (hence of producers). The agents belonging to a given cluster either use similar input(s), supply similar product(s) or interchange intermediary products.

Since commodity-space encompasses both goods and services, dated and located, this topological notion of a cluster of cones in R^l yields actually the central concept of an industrial subsystem that includes de facto manufacturers, alongside business partners such as bankers, suppliers, retailers, industry-related services, as well as the Government through public institutions, utilities and the policy environment in general.

A regular consultative process between members of a subsystem clearly increases the flow of information within that subsystem. It also channels to the members of the group external information on subregional or international variables. It therefore reduces the variance σ_j that distorts j's perception of the price system.

The strategy adopted through such a process may be viewed as the outcome of a non-cooperative game. One can prove that under these assumptions, it is Pareto-superior to individual strategies. (Loosely speaking, each agent belonging to the subsystem could always act as though he did not know the information obtained through the game, and thus resume his initial position with its corresponding outcome.)

It is worth noting finally that the benefit derived from a subsystem rational strategy versus individual strategies is entirely independent of whatever externalities in production sets, since the latter singularities have been explicitly ruled out of the model in this first section.

An Interactive Decision-making Process for Policy Formulation

To achieve an effective symbiosis with a market's overall environment, industrial policy formulation must be aimed at building or strengthening the competitive position of domestic manufacturing lines.

This calls for concerted efforts in industrial enterprises, the industrial environment and the State's industrial policies, involving a clear and open identification of objectives and a broad consensus on the ways and means of achieving them.

The State's ultimate objective is usually equitable economic and social development, even if its margin for manoeuvre is frequently limited in practice by more pressing concerns such as public finances or the balance of payments. Private agents, on the other hand, may seek to enlarge their market share and increase profits or turnover.

However disparate, these objectives are not mutually exclusive nor incompatible: negotiations between the State and economic operators must lead to delineating interests on which everyone involved will concentrate their efforts. In the case of a market economy in an increasingly global environment, achieving these objectives is indissociable from strengthening the country's competitiveness.

An operational strategy for attaining such objectives must first identify obstacles to competitiveness: obsolescent production capacity, lack of venture capital required for the creation of small and medium-scale enterprises, general weakness of the institutional environment or bad economic policies.

The true obstacles, of course, often derive from an adverse combination of several constraints. Yet in order to focus the efforts made and to reinforce their impact, those constraints that operate in the short term must be clearly singled out.

At this stage, and in the absence of full information circulating freely among the agents involved, close cooperation is essential as a second-best alternative. The development and implementation of concerted industrial strategies is something of a sequential process here, whereby improvements in competitiveness are achieved incrementally as existing constraints are gradually overturned.

In order to achieve tangible results rapidly, the industrial and other entrepreneurial sectors, institutions and the government services directly affected must participate in the consultations. These must thus evolve from a select cluster of industry executives, bankers and high-level officials who have the greatest decision-making power in the sector concerned. Together, these individuals will work out a strategic analysis of the manufacturing activity with which they are all concerned. They will identify its advantages and disadvantages and use them to develop an integrated programme of action.

The benefits to be derived from such concerted actions will be collectively greater than those from the alternative scenario where the various operators formulate their strategies and policies in a purely independent fashion. Yet like any sensible, not particularly altruistic, economic agent, each participant will certainly compare his private, individual gains under either one of the two alternatives. He will eventually take active part in the consultations only if he directly benefits from them, regardless of the collective outcome.

Thus the consultations are prone to deviant behaviour on the part of agents, in so far as one individual may be tempted to adulterate the strategic information he reveals in the hope of deriving greater advantage for himself. For example, a private entrepreneur may deliberately overlook his firm's low technical productivity while complaining of unbearable fiscal pressure to justify its poor economic performance. The prevention of the moral hazard problem calls for careful incentive-compatible revelation mechanisms.

Consultations are then crucial to sustaining industrial development in economies that suffer from a lack of organization, or which are engaged in reforms targetting the very roots of the production system. The process is a complex one which, in order to be successful, must focus on concrete problems to which it will seek pragmatic solutions.

Such a consensus-building process must be furthermore closely monitored by a – formal or informal – body or institution endowed with three fundamental functions:

- *Mediation*, or neutral moderation, facilitating the launching and conduct of negotiations among agents that initially will be unaccustomed to, and are actually likely to resist, open and constructive dialogue;

- *Analysis*, so that the discussion is fuelled by objective, quantitative elements and results in the formulation of specific measures, and, above all, so that the diversionary tactics mentioned above are averted;

- *Action*, through close relations with decision-making circles in order to establish the credibility of the consultations as an effective instrument for the formulation and implementation of industrial strategies.

This organizational capacity does not have to reside in an institution created specifically for this purpose. On the contrary, it would be better if it developed in a flexible, even informal, manner by common accord between the State and economic operators and possibly with support from existing institutions, federations or unions whose efficacy has already been demonstrated.

The Emerging Government-Industry Relationship

While the economic changes now taking place indicate an overall withdrawal of the State from productive activities, it would be misleading to assume that the Government's role in economic management is being commensurately reduced. True, the State's new responsibilities are fundamentally different from its old mandate in the centralized system, but they call for greatly strengthened analytical and regulatory capacities. In industrialized and developing countries alike, reform of public finances has caused substantial reductions in government sector employment; in developing countries, these measures are compounded by serious salary gaps between the public and private sectors and an insidious lack of motivation among government employees, resulting in a significant impoverishment of the State's human resources precisely when the national economy is undergoing radical changes.

In any event, one can currently distinguish four functions, or rather categories of functions, that a modern State may be expected to undertake in a market set-up (some of these points have been raised in earlier chapters and are merely touched on here):

- *Support to strengthening enterprise competitiveness*

   The State, by introducing the necessary industrial policy measures, must be the main agent in the development or strengthening of local industry's ability to cope successfully with international competition. The very notion of industrial policy is sometimes anathema to the authorities of economies in transition, who see therein the spectre of the centralized excesses of the past.

   Whatever the underlying ideological considerations, it is clear that, if only by its intrinsic weight or its authority on the international scene, the State will go on influencing the market. There is little doubt, however, that the very approach of selective interventionism by the State, which arguably looms large behind the East Asian Miracle, is prone to considerable external pressure in the post-GATT era. The recent trade dispute between Japan and the United States over alleged discriminatory practices in the Japanese market for photographic films (Fuji vs. Kodak, June 1995), is a case in point. The Japanese side reckons that the sector did benefit from strong – if temporary – government support during the 1960s and 1970s, when tariffs up to 40 per cent were levied on imported substitutes to protect the nascent local industry. Clearly such a policy would not be sustainable today, as it would quickly trigger an appeal to the World Trade Organization.

- *Management of public enterprises*

   A number of factors indicate that, even after the current transitional process has ended, the State will retain some of its functions in government enterprise management. These factors include:

- Lack of local savings and a domestic capital market;
- Absence of legislation governing property rights and enterprise creation or enterprise liquidation procedures;
- The social cost of overly rapid privatization, owing in particular to the direct and indirect impact of job reduction;
- The strategic nature of some industries, though this is a somewhat hackneyed term reflecting merely the State's natural reticence towards the privatization process.

Even if the trend points towards a sharp decline, the State will clearly continue to participate in productive activities for many years to come. It is therefore necessary to create a system of incentives that can serve as a de facto substitute for the private economy. Such incentives will make administrative officers in government enterprises face the consequences of their actions and will influence the decisions they take through signals comparable to the natural effect of market forces. Thus, in the case of the performance contracts mentioned earlier (see Chapter 3), administrative officers will receive bonuses if the enterprise's performance attains pre-established targets. Choosing the targets and determining the nature and size of the incentives is in itself a complex procedure which, experience has shown, can rapidly yield improvements in the economic efficiency of government enterprises.

• *Monitoring the privatization process*

The most visible of the State's functions in any economy in transition remains the institution and supervision, in a variety of ways, of the privatization process. A number of crucial points can be derived here from the experience of various countries:

- Looking beyond the budgetary year: Privatization is too often considered from a narrow, short-term standpoint, as a way of increasing the State's revenue and, by so doing, of balancing the budget. These direct consequences of privatization are, of course, crucial for countries with large public deficits but should not overshadow the benefits in the longer term, when market forces will automatically oblige the newly privatized enterprises to adjust their production structures in line with a more efficient use of available resources.

– Creation of monopolies: In countries where the distribution of national wealth is patently inequitable, domestic investment capacity is confined to a handful of privileged families. Privatization in such cases can greatly amplify industrial concentration and thus work against the consumer. In the Philippines, for example, the recently (re)privatization of the cement industry resulted in an oligopolistic market structure, at a time of highly profitable opportunities when construction is booming.

– The role of foreign investment: One way of preventing the development of domestic monopolies is to open the capital of privatized enterprises to foreign investment. This practice usually results in higher bids and, by generating partnerships, promotes the transfer of technology and managerial competence. Some countries with a low level of domestic savings experience foreign investment as a form of economic invasion and adopt measures specifically designed to restrict it. Moreover, some forms of foreign capital inflows such as portfolio investments, when not carefully regulated, may lead to domestic inflation and a risky exposure to the vagaries of emerging markets in general.

– Equity and social impact: As mentioned earlier, privatization should help to distribute more equitably the ownership of the means of production. Marginal propensity to consume being generally higher for people in lower-income categories, there is a definite danger that workers will rapidly collect on their share of capital and even sell it back to enterprise managers, for whom the choice between consumption and investment poses less of a dilemma. Some privatizations carried out through repurchase of the enterprise by its workers have turned out to be de facto take-overs by managerial staff. Social relevance in general is intimately linked in the public mind to possible job losses and reduced revenue, although here, too, it is difficult to draw final conclusions on the basis of foreign experience.[7] In many cases, however, the lost jobs reappear in more durable form in private enterprises.

- One cannot over-emphasize the importance of a legal, institutional and financial framework, though establishing one undoubtedly constitutes the principal challenge of the privatization process.

• *The State as regulator*

When economic reforms are specifically aimed at fairly rapid abolition of the formerly generalized price controls and other types of public sector interference, such as the often discretionary granting of sales and investment licences, the State as regulator may seem an anachronistic notion. Yet it is of crucial importance for preserving a competitive environment and countering the diversionary tactics that will all too soon emerge. Indeed the enterprise can react to increasing competition, in one of two ways: face the competition and seek to adapt dynamically to the new performance thresholds it requires, or try to avoid it by diverse and, in many cases, devious methods. Theoretical approaches have been somewhat idealistic, merely entertaining the first hypothesis. Empirical evidence on the other hand underlines the great importance of the second.

In the interests of consumers and of the public at large, the State must constantly seek to ensure that the rules of the game are respected and that market forces function effectively. To play this essential role, the State requires sharp expertise in modern industrial economics, to enable it to anticipate, assess and control attempts to undermine competition. The following points may be noted in this connection:

- Anti-dumping legislation: The recent conclusion of the GATT accords entails a general reduction in the protective tariffs that have indubitably impeded international trade. A less tangible measure, but one that will be equally beneficial to international trade – and especially, in all likelihood, to the developing countries – is the gradual eradication of dumping, by which an export price is made inferior to the original cost through price discrimination and cross-subsidization between domestic markets and exports or through generous State subsidies. For the importing country, this practice is akin to a negative effective protection; it creates the same price distortions between imported goods and domestic products and adversely modifies the market signals.

- Anti-monopoly legislation: The emphasis placed on anti-trust measures by the founders of the European Union is significant in this regard. Clearly, the founders expected that market integration would require a number of safeguards to be adopted. Yet there are no objective, undisputable indicators that would establish the actual prevalence of monopolistic practices or of dominant influence in a given market. Instead, disputes are treated on a case-by-case basis, often requiring the analysis of complex documentation in which legal points, jurisprudence and analysis of industrial organization are intermingled.

- Market specialization strategies: Owing to the need to adjust to increased competition, enterprises frequently withdraw from peripheral activities to concentrate, often heavily, on their core businesses where they enjoy solid comparative advantages. The trend is thus pointing towards ever stronger market concentration, over ever sharper segments of the manufacturing activities. This suggests that there is no fundamental difference between classical cost-competition and niche strategies. In other words, there is a continuum of the firm's behaviour of which the pure niche strategy is but an asymptotic case. Finally, it highlights the regulator's difficulty in distinguishing between the normal strategy of an enterprise in a competitive environment and an attempt to abuse a dominant market position.

- Quality standards: One observes in practice three modes of reaction by enterprises to new exigencies in the area of quality. The first, a neutral reaction, is passive compliance with international quality standards. The second, or positive, reaction is when quality is taken as a strategic variable on the same terms as price or customer service and made into a definite selling point. The third type of reaction likewise uses quality as a strategic variable, but for negative purposes: ever higher and costlier standards of quality are posted in an attempt to deter market entry or to inhibit competition. There is a slim borderline, easily traversed, between the second and third types of reaction: preventing abuse of quality standards calls for finely honed analytical capacities and looms large, in fact, among the objectives for the World Trade Organization.

- The environment: Here one faces the same types of reaction from enterprises, including a diversionary tactic whereby the ecological, or 'green' label, is used to block the entry of potential competitors into specific segments of the market.
- Dubious employment practices: An enterprise may seek to reduce its manufacturing costs either by boosting productivity and opting for better production techniques or by reducing input costs. In developing countries, where salaries account for a considerable portion of manufacturing value added and where labour legislation is somewhat weak, heads of enterprises are under great temptation to cut money wages to the minimum. Such wage competition, which to a large extent shapes foreign investment patterns in South-East Asia, keeps the earnings of workers and the purchasing power of households very low and therefore appears at variance with the social objectives of economic development.

Notes

1. In the jargon of game theory introduced in subsequent paragraphs, the central planning approach is referred to as one-sided game, or game of 'Government vs. Nature'.
2. Or for that matter, the resurgence of communist regimes in eastern Europe.
3. However, one observes in western countries a gradual stabilization of the pendulum between the two dialectic poles.
4. As opposed to a coerced convergence that is found when a somewhat weaker risk of popular sanction through the electoral process paves the way for a collusive behaviour between Government and employers.
5. In a General Equilibrum or at the limit of a 'Global' Equilibrum framework, assessment of p includes, for instance, the identification of market niches, new products, etc.
6. The analysis here will focus on prices, although an unprecise grasp of the available technology (a very common phenomenon in developing countries) will also entail inefficiencies. However, since y_j is likely to be in that case an interior point of Y_j, Y_j is not a binding constraint and thus, an accurate depiction of technological opportunities is not required.
7. The recent study by the World Bank and Boston University notwithstanding – see Chapter 3.

References

Amsden, Alice H. (1989), *Asia's next giant: South Korea and late industrialization*, Oxford University Press, New York.

Amsden, Alice H. (1993), 'A theory of Government intervention in late industrialization', in L. Putterman and D. Rueschemeyer (eds), *The State and the market in development*, Lynn Rienner.

Cornet, Bernard and Henry Tulkens (eds) 1989, *Contributions to operations research and econometrics: The twentieth anniversary of CORE*, MIT Press, Cambridge MA.

Debreu, Gérard (1959), *Theory of value: An axiomatic analysis of economic equilibrium*, John Wiley, New York.

Drèze, Jacques H. (1974), 'Econometrics and decision theory', in S. E. Fienberg and A. Zellner (eds), *Studies in Bayesian econometrics and statistics*, North-Holland, 1974.

Drèze, Jacques H. (1987), *Essays on Economic Decisions under Uncertainty*, Cambridge University Press, Cambridge, UK.

Lall, Sanjaya (1989), 'Building industrial competitiveness in developing countries', *Development Centre Studies*, OECD, August.

Scholtès, Philippe R. (1993), 'Formulating industrial strategies and policies in the context of restructuring economies: Some preliminary thoughts', *Industry and Development No. 33*, UNIDO.

Smith, Stephen C. (1991), 'Industrial policy in developing countries: Reconsidering the real sources of export-led growth', *Economic Policy Institute*, Washington, D.C.

Tirole, Jean (1988), *The theory of industrial organization*, MIT Press, Cambridge MA.

Wade, Robert (1990), *Governing the market: Economic theory and the role of Government in East Asian industrialization*, Princeton University Press, Princeton NJ.

World Bank (1991), 'The reform of public sector mangement: Lessons from experience', *Policy and Research Series*, Washington, D.C.

World Bank (1993), *The East Asian miracle: Economic growth and public policy*, Oxford University Press, New York.

World Bank (1995), *Global Economic Prospects and the Developing Countries*, Washington, D.C.

6. Capital Inflows and Technology Transfers in Developing Countries

*Philippe R. Scholtès**

Introduction: the Driving Forces of Globalization

Over the past 30 years, the steady expansion of international trade for goods and services, on average, has outpaced the growth of global output. More significant still, soaring flows of foreign direct investment in the global scene have since the early 1980s outrun international trade expansion by a factor of three to four. The relative growth of external trade and foreign investment *vis-à-vis* production reflects the increased globalization of economic activities. Taken at the national level, the same indicators measure the degree of integration of a particular country into the international market place.

The tighter consolidation of manufacturing processes worldwide has been triggered by lower transportation costs, faster and more reliable communications and technological innovations allowing for increased specialization of production patterns. In addition, lower barriers to trade, domestic liberalization policies and international deregulation of capital markets and business services such as banking and insurance have considerably lessened the significance of national boundaries in resource allocation and blurred the former distinction between tradables and non-tradables.

Finally, production capacities and, more generally, technological capabilities have been remarkably strengthened in a number of developing

*United Nations Industrial Development Organization, Vienna. Paper prepared for UNIDO's Global forum on industry: Perspectives for the year 2000 and beyond (New Delhi, India, 16-18 October 1995). Contributions by Erich Gundlach and Peter Nunnenkamp of the Kiel Institute of World Economics, Nagesh Kumar of the United Nations Institute for New Technologies in Maastricht, and Sanjaya Lall of Oxford University are gratefully acknowledged.

countries. Combined with specific patterns of factor endowments and relative prices in those countries, they create opportunities for cross-border cooperation schemes and in the process alleviate the technology constraint in the firms' profit maximization behaviour.

These supply-side considerations should not obviate, however, specific policy reforms implemented by developing countries to spur capital inflows, improve the overall debt-equity exposure, keep up with the pace of technological progress and strengthen the competitiveness of their industries. Ultimately the nature and magnitude of capital flows to any given country will be determined by corporate strategies as well as by the attractiveness of the host economy. International competition for foreign capital is keen; Governments and local businesses must join forces to create dynamic comparative advantages if they are to capture an adequate share of world capital flows.

Forms of Globalization at the Process Level

Globalization at the process level of processes involves a transfer of technology in a broad sense, that is, encompassing capital goods, services such as training or management consulting and intangibles such as proprietary designs or brand names. These components of technology transfers in general are combined in different bundles and translate in practice into a variety of vehicles of global integration as follows:

- Pure *trade* in capital goods stands at one end of the spectrum. However, the range of technologies strictly available off the shelf is narrow, and its use confined to basic manufacturing processes. More important in the trade category is the extent of intra-firm trade of semi-transformed products between transnational corporations (TNCs) and their affiliates, estimated at about half of total world trade.[1] Although indicating a form of integration of manufacturing patterns in different countries, such arm's length exchanges of goods and services clearly play a marginal role as far as technology transfers are concerned.
- *Foreign direct investment* (FDI) still lies in the mainstream of cross-border cooperation between firms. It implies by definition the acquisition of majority stakes in host countries' enterprises and leads therefore to a redistribution of ownership and

control at the international level. An FDI package typically includes capital goods together with related services and intangible assets.

- *Non-equity cooperation* (NEC) on the contrary refers to a variety of international partnership forms where the foreign company does not explicitly seek control over the local enterprise. Through a NEC partnership, a bundle of tangible and/or intangible assets is provided by the foreign company to the local enterprise. Practical modes of non-equity cooperation are:

  - *Arm's length licensing* of technology, where the parent company grants access to designs, drawings or process know-how against royalties or a lump-sum licence fee: Restrictive clauses may figure in the contract, such as a limited time frame and stringent conditions on inputs or markets.

  - *Franchising*, or a form of licensing accompanied with the right to exploit locally brand names and trademarks: *Turnkey projects* refer to a full package of disembodied technology.

  - *Production sharing agreements* through international subcontracting on the basis of specifications imposed by the parent company: Agreements of this nature are considered under the inter-firm technology transfer category to the extent that they also include the delivery of proprietary designs and drawings.

  - *Strategic technology alliances* cemented around joint research and development and other innovative activities: They seal arrangements for two-way transfers of technology.

  - *Joint ventures* with minor foreign equity stakes: Like FDI, they suggest a financial participation in the capital of the host company, although restricted here to a minority one (typically limited to 10–20 per cent of the capital).[2]

  - *Portfolio investment*, or the acquisition by foreign investors of minority stakes in local enterprises. Portfolio investments today account for a fast-growing share of global capital flows. Unlike joint ventures, they do not necessarily entail a transfer of technology, but can remain a purely financial operation; it is primarily a balance-of-payment concept.

Trends

This section presents empirical trends in international capital flows, while the next sections will attempt to analyse corporate strategies as well as policy measures.

International patterns of inter-firm cooperation can be observed from a number of angles, each one of them offering useful insights into the underlying rationale and mechanisms. A technical caveat must however be kept in mind throughout this exercise: it hints at the difficulty of ensuring consistency in the treatment of different forms of globalization. While FDI can be traced from flows of goods, services and incomes in balance-of-payment statistics, NEC-related data are diluted into broader aggregates and are thus not directly available. An alternative source of information is found in ad hoc databases such as records of technology receipts by industrialized countries or MERIT[3] which monitors over 10,000 collaborative ventures world-wide. The patterns are as follows:

- *Evolution over time*: Arm's length contracts and other licensing arrangements accounted, until the early 1980s, for the bulk of cross-border technology transfers. A range of mature and stand-ard technologies came on stream at that time, enlarging global production capacities and offering new opportunities for cross-border partnerships. Through fear of foreign dominance and ex-cessive competition in their industrial sector, as well as being wary of a growing burden of remittances, Governments mean-while were imposing restrictions on FDI inflows, ranging from outright prohibition in certain sectors to local content require-ments and export obligation.

  International deregulation, domestic liberalization policies and privatization programmes in the early 1980s paved the way for a dramatic expansion of FDI flows. The rising trend was com-pounded by the rapid integration drive among European firms, by the launching of debt-equity conversion schemes in Latin America, as well as by a general recovery from the turmoil of the international debt crisis during the previous decade. Consolidated FDI flows grew from US$ 5 billion in 1980, to US$ 78 billion in 1994 (see Table 6.1), and they appear poised for further growth along the global integration thrust.

Finally, portfolio investments have staged a phenomenal growth since their first appearance on the world scene in the mid-1980s. However their former appeal as a high-yield financial instrument has been seriously undermined by the 1994 Mexican crisis, and it will probably take considerable time for them to reclaim their place in the portfolios of institutional investors and mutual fund managers.

- *Geographical distribution*: International collaborative ventures in the manufacturing sector of developing countries have been heavily skewed – and increasingly so – towards East Asia. In 1980, the East Asia and Pacific region attracted 31 per cent of total FDI, and 53 per cent of total portfolio investment flows. By 1994, the corresponding figures where 55 per cent and 45 per cent, respectively (ratios calculated from Table 6.2). Combined FDI and portfolio investments to East Asia grew from 32 per cent in 1987 to 53 per cent in 1994. Over the same period, the comparable shares of Latin America and sub-Saharan Africa decreased from 38 per cent to 25 per cent and from 9 per cent to 2 per cent, respectively.

Apart from portfolio investments, non-equity forms of cooperation are more difficult to apprehend in their evolving scope and magnitude, for reasons cited above. Yet sampling evidence clearly underlines the success of East and South-East Asia in capturing a large share of NEC flows aimed at developing countries. As for their strategic alliance component, it remains of marginal significance in developing countries, which secured less than 5 per cent of world collaborative ventures in R&D between 1980 and 1989.

There is growing concern that the increased concentration of FDI flows into a handful a developing countries will in effect lead to a technology drift in less favoured nations. Until the early 1980s, the 10 largest recipients of FDI channelled two thirds of the total flows to developing countries. By 1993, the figure had risen to 81 per cent. Arguably the composition of the top group has not remained invariant over the period – notably with China joining the club during the 1980s and quickly progressing to the top position – although the changes should not be exaggerated: a core group of 6 countries has constantly been in the top 10 since the early 1970s.

Table 6.1 Aggregate net resource flows by region
(US$ million)

	1970	1980	1987	1988	1989	1990	1991	1992	1993	1994
East Asia and the Pacific	2,133	13,145	6,719	17,827	25,412	29,811	34,080	51,583	74,144	90,433
Europe and central Asia	622	17,056	10,235	6,118	12,094	18,467	21,281	35,858	41,084	40,642
Latin America and the Caribbean	4,184	30,179	13,893	15,365	7,926	20,347	29,877	32,071	63,499	43,301
Southern Asia	1,329	6,371	10,373	12,515	11,390	9,569	11,831	8,286	11,509	18,841
Sub-Saharan Africa	1,644	15,146	14,566	14,279	18,090	16,606	16,047	16,978	15,675	21,897
Western Asia and North Africa	1,152	8,417	12,533	11,245	9,505	8,653	11,338	8,119	7,199	12,211
All developing countries	11,063	90,314	68,537	77,447	84,493	103,489	124,707	153,031	213,110	227,323

Source: World Debt Tables 1994–1995.

Table 6.2 Net resource flows by region and type of instrument: 1987 and 1994
(US$ million)

	1987				1994			
	Debt	FDI	Portfolio	Grants	Debt	FDI	Portfolio	Grants
East Asia and the Pacific	(187)	4,509	405	1,992	27,350	42,717	17,585	2,781
Europe and central Asia	8,702	1,302	79	151	20,015	11,134	2,549	6,944
Latin America and the Caribbean	5,878	5,791	278	2,146	11,465	18,875	10,438	2,523
Southern Asia	7,384	410	–	2,580	7,460	845	7,726	2,810
Sub-Saharan Africa	6,081	1,405	–	7,080	6,331	2,241	803	12,522
Western Asia and North Africa	8,429	1,160	–	2,964	6,850	2,107	350	2,904
All developing countries	36,287	14,576	761	16,913	79,471	77,918	39,450	30,484

Source: World Debt Tables 1994–1995.

Finally, a relatively new development in this arena is the so-called 'flying geese pattern' in Asia, where outward-bound FDI flows are on the rise and are increasingly aimed at industrialized countries.

* *Breakdown by industry*: Different industries rely on different technology bundles, incorporating varying combinations of intangibles and tacit components. Consequently, the extent and shape of cross-border cooperation between firms is expected to be highly industry specific.

The textile and clothing industry is characterized by a relatively high – though decreasing – labour intensity, a rather low level of technological sophistication and processes that easily lend themselves to fragmentation. The industry is therefore widely dispersed internationally. Inter-firm cooperation mostly takes the shape of non-equity arrangements, and despite restrictive policies under the Multi-Fibre Agreement, in 1993 developing countries contributed 35 per cent of global textile output and 26.4 per cent of world production of clothing (UNIDO database).

The production of chemicals on the contrary is a typically capital-intensive industry. The market is dominated by a few OECD-based TNCs, which together account for a large share of world total output. Mostly driven by these TNCs, FDI flows to developing countries resulted in the region producing in 1993 as much as 18 per cent of the global output of industrial chemicals, while NEC schemes were particularly prevalent in the petrochemicals sector. Because of its strong R&D content and the importance of innovation, the pharmaceuticals industry has not been so pervasive in developing countries.

On the other end of the spectrum, the new core technologies comprising biotechnology, composite materials and information technology are extremely dependent upon massive investments in research and development. The high technology and extreme specialization characterizing these sectors fuelled intense research partnerships in the form of strategic alliances. In a survey of over 4,000 strategic alliances concluded worldwide during the 1980s, MERIT researchers found that 75 per cent of them originated in the field of new technologies. Not surprisingly, most of those were technology-oriented, rather than production- or market-oriented, and nearly all involved only industrialized countries.

Corporate Strategies and Instruments

As for any economic exchange, cross-border inter-firm cooperation eventually results from a convergence of interests between two agents, namely here a foreign and a local partner. Loosely speaking, firms tend to maximize their profits (in a broad sense) and see in overseas markets opportunities to generate revenues or to reduce production costs. Local enterprises in host countries rely on foreign transfers to alleviate capital shortages or to catch up with international technology levels. In between, Governments intervene in an attempt to regulate the process, for various considerations. The outcome of the strategic game between these three interest groups ultimately determines the form, scope and magnitude of globalization patterns in the manufacturing sector.

- Corporate strategies behind *foreign direct investment* fall under four broad categories:

  - *Market penetration* has always been a prime motivation underpinning FDI flows to developing countries, and particularly to those with a large population and sizable purchasing power. As such, FDI can become an effective instrument to circumvent restrictive trade policies in the host country.
  - FDI is also an important vehicle to enhance the *efficiency of manufacturing* processes by taking advantage of differentials across countries in resource and factor endorsements. This aspect permeates FDI flows to East and South-East Asia, regions characterized by a large pool of relatively skilled manpower as well as a strong technological base, by developing countries' standards. It also underscores recent Japanese investments in Europe and the United States, seen partly as a way of hedging against a strong domestic currency that adversely affects the profitability of export-oriented manufacturing.
  - Trade supporting FDI is resorted to when the *expansion of sales* in a foreign market critically hinges upon a close relationship with the clientele in order to offer customized products, a far-reaching marketing network or attractive after-sale services. The growing outflow of FDI from Asia to industrialized countries appears, to a significant extent, driven by such considerations.

    – Finally, firms may exploit the FDI vehicle to acquire *strategic assets* in foreign countries and to benefit in the process from bundled intangibles such as possible knowledge spillovers, technology or brand names.

• Similarly, non-equity forms of cooperation are prompted by corporate objectives such as penetrating a new market, exploiting complementary technologies or accelerating the pace of innovation (such motivations together account for 80 per cent of all inter-firm cooperation agreements, according to the MERIT database).

The recourse to either form of cross-border partnership is by-and-large determined by the local conditions in the host country.[4] Owners of intangibles such as technology, know-how or brand name strive to extract maximum revenue out of their assets. Outright sale or licensing is sometimes impeded by valuation problems, due to the necessity to account for possible externalities and the risk of dissipation of brand goodwill, but also because of the necessary codification of knowledge and the inherent reluctance of the seller to fully disclose the object of the bargaining process.

Thus transaction costs exert a strong influence on the ultimate shape of the technology transfer. They clearly vary across industries, along with the particular bundle of intangible assets embedded in different technologies. The higher the transaction costs, the stronger the incentives to internalize the exchange by resorting to FDI rather than NEC instruments. For instance, the valuation of product-related ownership advantages such as brand names or differentiated goods is fraught with uncertainty, due to significant externalities. In this case, firms will favour the FDI channel to realize their intangible assets. When capitalizing on process-related assets, TNCs will use arm's length contracts for standardized and relatively simple technologies, while they will tend to prefer the FDI alternative for manufacturing process displaying a large R&D content, or calling for highly specialized skills.

NEC is also seen as an alternative to FDI by risk-averse investors who limit their stakes in the host company by fear of local turmoil and possible expropriation. By the same argument, non-equity participation in small-scale industries is a viable option in terms of containing the risk associated with more volatile partners.

Finally, portfolio investments appear poised to stand out in the near future as a prime source of capital flows. Yet such capital flows are mostly driven by institutional investors and managers of mutual funds for their attractive yield/risk ratios and the scope they offer for a wide geographical diversification of assets. Therefore, their contribution to the globalization trend is essentially that of mobilizing a large pool of finance, particularly valuable to small and medium enterprises in emerging markets.

Implications for Developing Countries

The significance of the globalization phenomenon has been well documented for industrialized countries, and figures prominently in the intense debate on persisting unemployment in those parts of the world. Indeed the growing competition from developing countries on the low-skilled segment of the labour market is seen as a major factor behind structural job losses in the blue-collar category. A somewhat extreme view on the subject[5] reckons that import competition from developing countries has reduced by as much as 20 per cent the demand for low-skilled labour in industrialized countries over the past three decades. However, empirical evidence suggests that the actual interactions between foreign trade and investments are very complex indeed, and OECD-specific factors such as productivity growth, technological change as well as migrations obviously loom large behind structural unemployment patterns. At any rate, policy options in rich countries are essentially of three orders: first, a relative depreciation of low-skilled wages; second, a drive to higher-skilled categories; and third, the rise of ever subtler protectionist measures.

The implications for developing countries are no doubt far-reaching, although difficult to assess with a satisfactory degree of accuracy. The ultimate gains from increased trade integration are expected to be unevenly distributed in the developing world. Likewise, the globalization of manufacturing processes stands to raise both challenges and opportunities in developing countries. As a matter of fact, challenges may often be turned into opportunities, provided the recipient country is able to wisely manage its capital inflows (see the following section). Indeed, the following list is attempted as a brief review of salient globalization-related issues; it highlights the close interaction between corporate strategies and government policies and in doing so, gradually introduces the final section of the chapter.

- A *greater integration into the world economy* is undoubtedly the major achievement of cross-border cooperation among firms. Greater integration in turn entails greater allocative efficiency by means of a price-consistent choice of factors on a global scale, a fuller exploitation of local comparative advantages and the ensuing rationalization of manufacturing processes. It also suggests greater distributive efficiency by virtue of the simultaneous expansion of markets and a diluted risk of dominant behaviour over a larger market base.

- *Easier access to new technologies* and a reduced time-lag between technological innovation and its penetration in developing countries are other direct benefits. Technology is increasingly drifting away from pure capital goods, and tends to include an ever greater intangible content by means of skills, know-how or organizational requirements. Thus its effective transfer to developing countries today calls for a close partnership between owners and users, whether through the exchange of majority stakes or by way of arm's length collaboration.

- The broader *availability of private development finance* is an important feature of FDI flows and portfolio investments alike. FDI alone accounted in 1992 for 4.9 per cent of the total gross fixed capital formation in developing countries, although the figure varies greatly across regions, from a low of 0.5 per cent in western Asia to a high of 5.5 per cent in southern, eastern and South-East Asia.[6] Private capital flows now far exceed official grants and aid (except in sub-Saharan Africa). They offer real financing opportunities to small and medium enterprises as well as to large infrastructural projects characterized by a high incremental capital-output ratio. As such they palliate the lack of venture capital and a typically shallow financial depth in developing countries.

- Aside from scope and magnitude aspects, *quality considerations* are also of the essence for a comprehensive assessment of capital inflows. Clearly the debt-equity swaps in Latin America or privatization-induced capital flows to Africa do not carry the same benefits as new investments in greenfield projects. Similarly, FDI attracted by the sheer market size of the host country merely exploits a natural endowment, while offshore manufacturing for re-exportation strives for the progressive accumulation of physical and human capabilities. Finally, while a liberal regime is expected to trigger FDI inflows and give faster access to foreign technologies, it may also inhibit a crucial technological deepening process at home. Japan and the Republic of Korea are outstanding examples of countries that closely monitored capital inflows and avoided an adverse crowding-out effect on their domestic market.

- There are fears of a looming *poverty trap* where the relative affluence of gradually industrializing countries will translate into higher wages and eventually result in manufacturing relocation in lower-income countries. The evolution of investment patterns in Asia is often cited as evidence to support this view. The argument overlooks the fundamental fact that real wage increases *per se* are not relevant, unless they outpace the concomitant rise in productivity. Germany boasts some of the world's highest wages in manufacturing, thanks to world-class productivity figures in the sector. A more likely scenario is thus a global equalization of factor prices that will eventually reach out to traditionally low-mobility factors such as labour, and real wages in developing countries will be allowed to rise at par with labour productivity gains.

- *Technological progress in OECD countries* is seen as potentially detrimental to developing countries: Research and development will aim at lessening the dependence on the relatively rare factor. Technologies will become increasingly capital-intensive, and even knowledge-intensive, thus creating entry barriers that will restrict the scope for inter-firm cooperation to a close group of advanced countries. The emergence of regional clusters such as those established by the North American Free Trade Agreement and the European Union is sometimes perceived as a threat to a true globalization that would create opportunities for developing countries as well. However, these worries appear far fetched inasmuch as they are not supported by empirical evidence. On the contrary, the highest growth rates have been experienced in countries that did not belong to any strong regional grouping, and the gradual shift in some regions towards capital-intensive processes creates on the contrary opportunities for others to exploit their comparative advantage in low-skilled labour and simpler technologies.

- Finally, an overriding concern is the *impact on the balance-of-payment* of a lax attitude *vis-à-vis* FDI and portfolio investments. Capital inflows exert a direct effect under that same heading of balance of payment and an indirect effect on the current-account position through outflows of incomes and remittances, while the end effect will be balanced either by increased exports or at the cost of deteriorating foreign exposure. The electronics and electrical machinery subsector has proven the driving force of the impressive manufacturing growth in Malaysia, but its overall impact on balance of payment remains negative today. Whether such compromise is sustainable depends on structural factors of the economy: that Malaysia could obviously afford it is no indication that the strategy would necessarily succeed elsewhere.

Policy Response

International cooperation among manufacturing enterprises evolves in what is essentially a seller's market: On the one side figure powerful transnational corporations, while on the other, a large number of developing countries engage in fierce competition to capture a fair share of capital flows and technology transfers. Thus the bargaining power of the recipient is *a priori* limited, but the attractiveness of the host country partner can be considerably enhanced by a conducive policy environment.

- At the *international level*, some authors[7] have suggested the recourse to international policy coordination as a civilized settlement of the prevailing cut-throat competition for international capital. Yet harmonization attempts of this kind would inevitably result in boosting the importance of purely locational assets and initial endowments, leaving disadvantaged regions with very dim prospects indeed. Furthermore such type of cross-country agreement would be prone to the fragility inherent in any cartel, that is, the risk of collapse when members find stand-alone strategies more profitable than their individual gains in the cartel strategy.

- At the *macroeconomic level*, sound monetary and fiscal policies will no doubt be favourably considered by foreign investors. Moderate inflation and stable exchange rates contribute to reduced investment risks, stronger productivity growth and higher capital yields altogether. Fiscal restraint in turn allows for containing inflation within acceptable levels. Tariffs reduction and import liberalization in general pave the way for a spontaneous export drive, compatible with WTO rules. In transition economies, the creation of a legal environment to govern land reform and defend property rights is also part of the necessary preconditions for increased capital flows.

- More specifically at the *industry level*, ad hoc measures aimed at regulating capital flows have proven by and large ineffective as they often drew a rapid corporate response in the form of substitute instruments. Thus policy support can basically assume two forms:[8]

  - *Functional interventions* are applicable across the board. They include, in general, the provision of a so-called enabling environment featuring adequate infrastructures, utilities, institutional support, banking, insurance and other business services and, most importantly, a comprehensive human development programme. They also relate, as far as capital inflows are concerned, to measures such as the promotion and facilitation of investors, non-selective performance or ownership requirements, guarantees and arbitration.
  - *Selective interventions* on the contrary target specific industries or segments of the economy. When aimed at fostering capital inflows, they typically encompass the entry screening and selectivity, perhaps outright prohibition in certain areas, discretionary conditions on FDI incentives and operations, performance requirements by activity and targeting of foreign partners.

The recourse to government interventions – particularly of a selective kind – in the market, warrants careful justification. Functional interventions are said to be market friendly in the sense that they basically circumvent market failures such as information gaps that prevent capital markets from operating efficiently, a risk-averse behaviour hindering the accumulation of much-needed venture capital, and the presence of externalities due to knowledge spillovers and technological linkages.

In addition, the proponents of the technological capabilities approach cite empirical evidence from the development of East Asian countries to support the need for selective interventions. Technological deepening, they argue, is essential to manufacturing growth and a successful integration into the global market place. Yet it is a risky and costly endeavour, compounded by a punitively slow learning process. Firms require time and resources to adjust to increased competitive pressures. A passive, encompassing policy will tend to lure foreign investment into areas of static comparative advantage, while a mix of functional and selective measures can steer capital inflows towards more complex activities and help create dynamic advantages.

Perhaps a cogent argument for a sensible degree of government selectivity can be found in the limited resource mobilization capacity that characterizes developing countries. Disadvantaged regions are excluded from the mainstream of international capital flows. To attract FDI in spite of their relatively bland features, they can endeavour to outbid competitors by offering a more generous package of incentives across the board, but the ultimate cost-effectiveness of the strategy may be seriously undermined. The only alternative appears to concentrate scarce domestic resources on those industries where measurable competitiveness gains can be achieved, thus burnishing their international attractiveness. The combined effects of domestic policies and foreign capital may in turn create dynamic comparative advantages in the host country that could not have emerged otherwise.

Notes

1. Kumar (1995); World Bank (1995/b).
2. Arguably the acquisition of a minority share may well give the foreign investor a controlling stake in the local firm if, for instance, the remaining stock is evenly distributed among a large number of shareholders.
3. Maastricht Economic Research Institute on Innovation and Technology.
4. Dunning (1977).
5. Wood (1994).

6. UNCTAD (1995).
7. Oman (1994).
8. Lall (1995).

References

Dunning, John H. (1977), 'Trade, location of economic activity and the multinational enterprises: A search for an eclectic approach', in Bertin Ohlin, Per O. Hesselborn and Per M. Wijkman (eds), *The international allocation of economic activity*, London, pp. 395–418.

Gökgür, Nilgün (1994), 'Emerging markets: The rising role of portfolio investments', Working Paper, Harvard Business School, June.

Gundlach, Erich and Peter Nunnenkamp (1995), 'Globalization of manufacturing activity: Evidence and implications for industrialization in developing countries', UNIDO, June.

Kumar, Nagesh (1995), 'International linkages, technology and exports of developing countries: Trends and policy implications', UNIDO, July.

Lall, Sanjaya (1989), 'Building industrial competitiveness in developing countries', *Development Centre Studies*, OECD, August.

Lall, Sanjaya (1995), 'Governments and industrialization: The role of policy interventions on competitiveness', UNIDO, July.

Oman, Charles (1994), 'Globalisation and regionalisation: The challenge for developing countries', *Development Centre Studies*, OECD, May.

UNCTAD (1995), 'Recent developments in international investment and transnational corporation', TB/B/ITNC/2, Geneva, February.

Wood, Adrian (1994), *North-South trade, employment and inequality: Changing fortunes in a skill driven world*, Oxford, Clarendon Press.

World Bank (1995/a), *World Debt Tables 1994–1995*, Washington, D.C.

World Bank (1995/b), *Global Economic Prospects and the Developing Countries*, Washington, D.C.

Part II

Prospects for Industrial Development in the Red River Delta (Viet Nam): a Case-Study

Philippe R. Scholtès[*]
Hai Nguyen Thanh[**]

[*]United Nations Industrial Development Organization, Vienna.
[**]Independent consultant, Brussels.

7. Premises

The Government of Viet Nam, through the State Planning Committee, invited UNIDO to assist in developing an industrial strategy for the Red River Delta (RRD) region, with a view to maximizing the contribution of the industrial sector to regional economic and social development. The outcome of this mission is to be used as input to the broader RRD Master Plan.

Background of the Report: the Red River Delta Master Plan

The project VIE/89/034 'Master Plan for the Red River Delta' was approved in October 1992, with an initial budget of US$ 2.9 million supported by the United Nations Development Programme (UNDP), and a government contribution of Vietnamese dong (D) 2.2 billion (later to be increased to D7.0 billion). It responded to a growing concern for socio-economic stabilization and a balanced economic development between the northern and southern parts of the country, and followed the appeal of the Seventh Party Congress (June 1991) towards taking full advantage of the potential of the Red River Delta.

Operations started in April 1993, led at a rapid pace by a multi-disciplinary group of foreign specialists and national experts. In addition, the project implementation also benefited from Core Counterpart Teams made of government officials who prepared background materials for the numerous items to be covered.

A draft Master Plan report was already released in December 1993 and submitted to the relevant authorities for consideration. Meanwhile, the experts proceeded throughout 1994 with the preparation of an impressively large number of background documents, both in English and in Vietnamese. As the project was slated for completion in April 1995, the aim was to produce in early 1995 a revised version of the consolidated Master Plan report, allowing for its finalization and submission to the Government within the original time frame.

Emerging Shortcomings

Arguably the project was designed, and later implemented, with a strong bias towards infrastructure (roads, ports, dykes and irrigation works) and a fuller realization of the agricultural potential in the RRD region. Soon enough, however, the absence of an industrial dimension in the Master Plan was perceived as a major shortcoming; the achievement of national self-sufficiency in agriculture had meanwhile shifted the emphasis of policy makers to the benefits of accelerated industrialization, backed by increasing flows of foreign capital.

In reaction to the draft Master Plan report of December 1993, the Government stressed the rationale to expand the scope of the project and encompass the industrial sector. It created to that effect an ad hoc Core Counterpart Team, which set to work in mid-1994. The first tripartite review meeting of March 1994, as well as a subsequent joint evaluation mission (May 1994), further reiterated the need to formally include the industry under the purview of the project. UNIDO was therefore called upon to provide such inputs into the overall Master Plan.

Scope of the Study

Early discussions with project staff suggested that UNIDO's contribution take the shape of a separate, self-contained document moulded along the broad outline of the overall Master Plan report, so as to facilitate the subsequent consolidation of the industry component into the whole.

Yet the industry component differs from the general spirit of the Master Plan in many respects. The worrying drift of the budget deficit (poised to increase in 1994 by 17 per cent over comparable 1993 figures) imposes a renewed restraint on public finances: as recently stated by the Prime Minister, public expenditures will be curbed and State investment outlays will be sharply focused. It appears likely therefore, and indeed desirable, that future public investment programmes aim at such typical strongholds of the State as physical infrastructure, education and poverty alleviation.

A number of such public investment opportunities – in roads, irrigation, energy, etc. – are documented in the Master Plan. As regards however the industrial sector, the progressive adherence to market principles would rather indicate a different path for the Government; the private sector should be left with greater initiative, encouraged to expand and prosper, and ought in particular to be spared the crowding out effect of massive public investment. The Government should concentrate on facilitating the emergence of private businesses in the industrial sector, through a combination of sensible economic policies and institutional support.

Thus the industry report includes a relatively large section devoted to the overall economic environment and institutional set-up, in so far as these will carry a determining impact on future private sector-led industrialization patterns. Furthermore, in view of the prevailing rapid evolution of major components of the economic policy, the very term 'planning' has to be cautiously interpreted here when applied to industrial development. The thrust of the Plan should no longer seek to allocate public resources to productive purposes in the manufacturing sector; it should rather aim at endowing the Government with the capabilities required to effectively promote and facilitate a sustainable industrialization process in the region. The dynamics of industrial development are complex indeed, and new constraints will undoubtedly emerge in the future; to fulfil its new role, the Government must be able to quickly respond to the new conditions and monitor the development process. It needs to develop a strong expertise in strategic planning.

8. Overall Policy, Regulatory and Institutional Framework

Ever since the launching of 'Doi Moi', the renovation policy in 1986, the Government of Viet Nam has made remarkable progress on the road to a market economy. The pace of transformation was still considerably accelerated in recent months when the United States waived its veto against multilateral lending in July 1993, fuelling a rapid inflow of foreign capital from IMF, the World Bank and the Asian Development Bank, in particular. The November 1993 donors' meeting in Paris pledged US$ 1.86 billion in aid, though a modest share of it has been actually disbursed so far (US$ 400 million in 1994). A few months afterwards, in February 1994, the United States also lifted its trade embargo *vis-à-vis* Viet Nam, allowing for the resumption of trade flows between the two countries, and for private United States investment for the first time after the fall of Saigon in 1975. Finally the recent Consultative Group Meeting held in Paris in November 1994 resulted in total pledges in excess of US$ 2 billion.

These external shocks, however beneficial they are for the country, cannot avoid exerting a severe disbalancing effect on a fragile economy such as Viet Nam's. At the same time, while moving resolutely ahead with its programme of reforms, the Government is extremely cautious to avoid strategic mistakes and constantly modifies, amends or fine-tunes essential pieces of legislation. The outcome is a complex set of policy decisions, laws and regulations that are confusing, at times contradictory, and which sorely lacks the stability and predictability required for long-term business planning.

The following sections propose a rapid survey of the overall business environment in Viet Nam, made of general policy guidelines and their practical enforcement modalities through regulations and institutions. The perspective is that of a potential – domestic or foreign – investor in the manufacturing sector concerned with domestic inflation and the external stability of the local currency, as well as with the laws, regulations and institutional set-up that condition long-term finance, investment and trade, and will, to a large extent, determine the profitability of his business venture.

Macroeconomic Policies

Monetary policy

The *exchange rate* has been very stable since late 1991. The rate is set through foreign exchange trading floors established in 1991 at Hanoi and Ho Chi Minh City. Significant discrepancies between supply and demand for convertible currencies trigger the intervention of the State Bank. As the inflation rate over the same period has been remarkably low, the consolidated interventions by the State Bank have remained modest altogether, peaking at US$ 200 million in 1993. Yet they adversely affected the country's foreign reserves, now covering barely two months of imports at the present rate. There is moreover a growing concern that the ensuing steady overvaluation of the national currency has started undermining the country's competitive strength on export markets. The Government apparently intends to adjust the rate by allowing a moderate sliding of the currency rather than by means of a one-step devaluation that would deter foreign investors and cripple efforts to contain the 'dollarization' of the economy.

Interest rates on both loans and deposits are determined by the State Bank of Viet Nam (SBVN), basically as a mark-up on the prevailing inflation rate to ensure that real rates would remain positive. SBVN sets a maximum rate, or rather a schedule of such rates, according to criteria that have considerably evolved over the last five years. In 1989, the rates were differentiated according to economic sectors; later (1990) they were linked to the type of borrower or depositor, and since 1993, they tend to reflect the intended use of borrowed resources, whether for fixed or working capital. Apart from the multiplicity of administered rates, an odd feature of the present schedule lies in its inverted nature. In 1993, the applicable rate on fixed capital was 1.2 per cent per month, as against 2.1 per cent per month for working capital. Clearly the prevailing structure does not reflect such basic considerations as maturity or risk premium; it introduces a bias against long-term lending operations and inevitably leads to a misallocation of scarce domestic savings. When the Government eased domestic credit in 1993 (which increased 58.7 per cent that year, in real terms), it fuelled a surge in imports (46.4 per cent at constant prices) that went, to a large extent, to consumer goods and contributed little to increasing the domestic stock of capital (investment in 1993 represented 19.4 per cent of GDP, against 16.7 per cent in 1992).

Inflation appears now to stabilize at remarkably low levels for an economy in transition. The price reforms introduced in 1989 abolished most price controls which, in effect, reconciled official and free market prices. From 82.7 per cent in 1991, the consumer price index fell to 37.7 per cent in 1992 and further to 8.3 per cent in 1993, and is expected to remain at around 15 per cent in 1994. Inflationary pressures built up in the easy credit policy of 1993 were mostly diverted abroad through increased imports, thanks to a parallel move of trade liberalization. In early 1994 however, the Government restricted domestic credit by imposing on the banks, credit ceilings, higher interest rates and larger reserve requirements. Further attempts to curb the threat of inflation include a severe cut in capital expenditures budgeted for 1994, while attractive instruments under the June 1994 Domestic Investment Law are expected by the end of the year to mop up $2 billion of idle liquidities and channel these to investment in infrastructure and industry. Finally, the Government cannot rely on money supply as a sharp instrument to control inflation as the country's financial depth remains low, and includes furthermore a large, though decreasing, exogenous component due to the dollarization phenomenon.

Fiscal policy

Taxation is mainly seen as a means to generate revenues for the budget, rather than as a policy instrument to encourage growth in particular economic activities. As a consequence, the relevant legislation has evolved little since 1989, when a package of fiscal reforms was introduced to diversify from former traditional sources of revenue, i.e. proceeds from the oil industry and transfers from SOEs.

Notwithstanding excise duties, natural resource tax and personal income tax that have but a modest impact in generating revenues for the State, the two main sources of income are the turnover tax, also known as the business income tax, and the profit tax. The latter carries very high rates, and allows no deduction when reinvesting profits. It is resented by entrepreneurs as a major disincentive. The former features a dozen different rates, as the Government attempts to alleviate the distortions and the overall burden on producers that a turnover tax inevitably entails through its cascading effect. Plans for a deep revision of the tax system are on the drawing board; they should aim at reducing the average tax rate, limiting the number of rates, alleviating present distortions in the structure and introducing perhaps a value-added tax to replace the turnover tax.

Tariffs and trade policy in general are on the contrary viewed as proactive policy tools to ensure an adequate balance between domestic production and imports to supply the local market, in addition to raising fiscal revenues. To spur exports, the Government offers duty drawbacks or full exemption on imported inputs processed for exportation. Recognizing, however, that an estimated four fifths of manpower still work for the domestic market, it also raises high tariffs to shelter the local import-substitution industry. The steady increases in tariffs are worrying, as they do not seem conducive to the development of sustainable manufacturing processes. They also stimulate large-scale smuggling. The total import duties collected in 1993 amounted to 15.8 per cent of the total value of imports, a figure that seems low compared to the tariff rates (even after considering the impact of duty exemptions and businesses under the export processing zone (EPZ) regime).

More important perhaps than the higher rates across the board is the emerging steeper gradient of the tariff schedule, which creates additional distortions and de facto introduces unwarranted rates of effective protection, far above the nominal rates. As an illustration, the tariff on automobiles was recently (1 July 1994) pushed to 200 per cent for the final product (up from 150 per cent), and to 40 per cent for the complete knock-down kit (up from 30 per cent). Assuming that the value-added in assembly represents 20 per cent of the cost of the components, the following effective protection rate for the assembly process can be inferred (see Table 8.1).

While this is arguably intended to protect the local automobile assembly industry, it results in granting this manufacturing process an effective rate of protection of 1,000 per cent. In other words, automobile assembly in Viet Nam is thereby allowed to be 10 times less efficient than foreign competitors, a major incentive for the local firms not to improve their productivity and build a competitive strength. The discrepancy between nominal and effective rates of protection would be even higher if the value-added in assembly turned out to be less than the assumed 20 per cent.

Table 8.1   An example of current effective protection in Viet Nam

	International price	Applicable tariff rate *(Effective protection)*	Domestic price *(Maximum price)*
Knocked-down kit	100	40%	140
Assembly	20	*1,000%*	220
Final product	120	200%	360

This clearly calls for a major revision of the present tariff structure, aimed at reducing the average rate, limiting the number of rates and setting these on the basis of the effective protection they entail. A thorough analysis of effective rates of protection in manufacturing would certainly prove most valuable if the Government is to design a sensible tariff schedule that truly maximizes the potential yield of domestic resources.

The Regulatory Framework

The legal environment
The mid-1980s have seen an impressive development of the legal framework in Viet Nam. The main building blocks of a business-friendly environment have been progressively assembled. The new constitution of 1992 recognizes property rights, the bankruptcy law of 1993 spells out the rights and liabilities of closing enterprises, allowing, *inter alia,* for accelerated liquidation and restructuring of public enterprises. The land law of the same year gives foreigners access to long-term (50–70 years) land use rights, although the right until now cannot be mortgaged to serve as collateral. The June 1994 domestic investment law includes a number of incentives to mobilize domestic savings, while the foreign investment law, enacted in December 1987, underwent several amendments to lure foreign savings into the country. The labour code of 1994 delineates employers' as well as workers' rights and duties enshrined in a labour contract. Further work on the lawmakers' agenda includes a commercial law and a consolidated civil code, both scheduled for 1995.

This impressive development of the legal body bears testimony to the determination of the authorities to proceed with the full implementation of economic reforms. The new set of laws remain however drafted in too general terms, and its actual enforcement typically calls for a complex, discriminatory – and discretionary – set of decrees and ordinances.

Trade regulations

The overall tariff structure was discussed earlier in the section on fiscal policy. While the tariff and revenue law of 1991, amended in July 1993, sets a range of acceptable rates, the actual rates that will eventually be enforced proceed from negotiations between the Ministry of Finance, the Ministry of Trade and, to some extent, the business community. Proposed rates are then submitted to the Government for possible endorsement. Applicable rates are furthermore subject to a quarterly review and possibly modified as part of the monitoring of budget revenues.

In addition, the Government through various ministries and agencies has the authority to issue or revoke import certificates, permits and licences, and the responsibility to grant duty drawbacks, outright exemptions or the full EPZ status. The outcome is a very complex and unpredictable web of rules and regulations which sorely lacks transparency and considerably lengthens foreign trade operations.

Investment regulations

Foreign investment is regulated by the law of December 1987, amended in 1990, 1992 and 1993. It considers essentially three types of foreign investment: joint ventures with a Vietnamese partner, wholly owned foreign company operating in Viet Nam (made possible by the 1993 amendment) and business cooperation agreements between existing foreign and local enterprises, without changing their legal status. It furthermore extends special privileges to particular forms of FDI, such as EPZs and BOT schemes, to entice overseas capital to developing a much needed infrastructure in Viet Nam. It does not consider yet the prospect of portfolio investment. There, also, investors resent the cumbersome procedures; they are weary of the multiplicity, complexity and volatility of the prevailing regulations. Loopholes such as the lack of an authorized translation for important pieces of legislation – such as the EPZ regime – renders the situation prone to abuses of discretionary power by the administration. In a survey by *Business Asia* (9 May 1994 issue), 40 per cent of a sample of potential investors called for a clarification and simplification of investment regulations as 'the single biggest thing the Government can do to improve the business climate'.

Nevertheless, FDI flows were impressive in 1993, at least at face value. Indeed the official figures reported by the State Committee for Cooperation and Investment (SCCI), the government agency that monitors foreign investment in the country, are believed to be grossly optimistic in many respects. First, they reflect intentions rather than formal commitments, and the implementation rate is actually low; second, they include the Vietnamese component in the case of joint ventures; and third, they include debt as well as equity financing. Business reports suggest that potential investors are in a stand-by mode, waiting for additional evidence of economic and administrative reforms.

Domestic investment is strongly encouraged in the recent (June 1994) domestic investment law, by means of preferential taxes and rules. The Government hopes to raise US$ 20 billion by the end of the decade from domestic sources to complement the US$ 25–30 billion expected from foreign sources – including a planned US$ 2 billion bond issue on international markets – over the same period. Attractive incentives are urgently required to bolster domestic savings and channel these into investment. Total investment in 1993 stood at 19.4 per cent of GDP, which set at 2.2 the incremental capital/output ratio (ICOR) of that year. This figure is unusually low, and indicates a high return – in terms of GDP growth – on investment, explained to a large extent by the low degree of capacity utilization and the high labour intensity prevailing in Viet Nam. This low ICOR is certainly not sustainable, and further GDP growth at the same pace will require increasingly massive investment flows.

Labour regulations

The absence of proper regulations, particularly in the non-State sector, bred growing labour unrest in the past two years across all categories of enterprises. A new labour law was passed through the National Assembly in June 1994. It represents a comprehensive piece of legislation that includes provisions on jobs, labour contracts, working and rest hours, occupational safety, women and child labour, social insurance, the role of trade unions, etc. Although it does not fix a minimum wage level, for the first time it recognizes and regulates the right to strike.

The Institutional Set-up

Financial institutions

Until recently, the banking industry in Viet Nam was heavily concentrated in four State-owned commercial banks (SOCB), that absorbed most of the deposits and accounted, at the end of 1993, for as much as 90 per cent of total outstanding credit. They are the Bank for Foreign Trade of Viet Nam (Vietcombank), the Bank for Investment and Development of Viet Nam (BIDV), the Industrial and Commercial Bank (Incombank, established in 1988) and the Viet Nam Bank for Agriculture (Agribank, also established in 1988).

The SOCBs clearly enjoyed the confidence of their clientele as the country avoided the severe disintermediation process typical of transition economies (the financial depth, although limited, has remained fairly stable since 1989). However, the role of these banks remain confined to money lending operations; they are not yet involved in improving corporate governance and hardening the budget constraint of SOEs.

A change in banking regulations in 1993 opened the door to foreign financial intermediaries: to date, 17 branches of foreign banks (4 from France, 3 from Thailand, 2 from the United States, and 1 each from Australia, Belgium, China, China (Taiwan Province), Germany, Netherlands, Republic of Korea and United Kingdom), 3 joint ventures with local banks, and 22 representative offices were operating in the country. If the Government wants to channel increased domestic savings to the banking sector, it needs also to encourage the creation of local, private banks and, to that end, correct the current tax regime applicable to the banking industry that effectively discriminates against equity-funded intermediaries. If it wants furthermore to channel these resources into long-term capital, it must also revise the present schedule of interest rates.

Investment promotion

Investment in the country is closely monitored by SCCI, which includes, *inter alia,* departments of law and investment promotion, project evaluation, export processing zones, as well as investment transaction centres at Hanoi and HCMC. It is also responsible for producing the influential weekly *Viet Nam Investment Review,* 'Viet Nam's first international business newspaper'. It is not, however, a one-stop window to foreign investment licensing, as the full process reportedly involves as many as eight central government agencies, local government authorities and SOEs if required.

SCCI and the State Planning Committee (SPC)[1] evaluate and review investment proposals against their own assessment of existing capacities, prevailing and projected supply and demand in that particular area, and determine on that basis whether the new investment is warranted. If so, they grant the necessary investment licence. The Ministry of Science, Technology and Environment (MOSTE) in turn intervenes to screen the technology involved in the project and its possible environmental impact. If satisfactory, MOSTE issues a technology licence. The concerned line ministry furthermore analyses the proposal *vis-à-vis* existing SOEs in this sector. As the line ministry until now remains directly responsible for the performance of SOEs under its supervision, it obviously has a vested interest to restrain competition on its turf.

As a result, foreign investors tend to favour the joint-venture option, preferably with a well-connected SOE. The greatest appeal of the expanding EPZ programme is likely to stem from its bureaucracy-free feature rather than from the various tax rebates it carries. SCCI has tried to alleviate the strong disincentive effect of this cumbersome procedure by licensing six investment service organizations, which offer to assist the potential investor through the process, and charge in return a fee of 0.3 per cent of the total investment.

External trade
Fortunately the procedures to engage in external trade are far simpler, particularly for manufacturing firms. The Ministry of Trade issues certificates for import/export activities, which have become automatically attached to the granting of foreign investment licences.

Other institutions
Although Viet Nam never had the overwhelming SOE sector typical of command economies, the country failed altogether to develop significant institutional support to non-State businesses. Heavy industry was, and remains, dominated by public enterprises which are directly managed by their line ministry and do not therefore justify particular institutional support. The non-State sector is found mostly in the light industry segment; it includes cooperatives (in constant regression since 1986), private enterprises (still timid with only 1,114 firms in 1992

(see Table A.5 in Annex)) and a booming private household sector. Thus the distribution of private productive units is very diffuse, and certainly hinders the effective provision of adequate institutional assistance.

The Viet Nam Chamber of Commerce and Industry, still limited in its membership (800 members in 1993), caters to the needs of both SOEs and private businesses and endeavours in particular to promote overseas trade and investment missions. The Central Council of Vietnamese Cooperatives and non-State Enterprises is an apex body created or rather revamped in 1991 that encompasses the Union of Supply and Marketing Cooperatives, the Union of Small Industry and Handicrafts Cooperatives, the Union of Construction Cooperatives, the Union of Transport Cooperatives, and associations of entrepreneurs and private enterprises. The Central Council conveys members' interests to the policy makers of the country and provides in addition a range of extension services.

The Non-State Economic Development Centre was established in 1991 to support the development of non-State enterprises of all kinds. Worth noting is the 60-year-old National Women's Union, which enjoys the backing of a strong membership (7 million) to look after the improvement of living standards of women through job creation.

Note

1. SCCI and SPC were, in late 1995, merged into a new ministry, the Ministry for Planning and Investment.

9. Resource Base and Current Manufacturing Patterns in the Red River Delta

Manufacturing Activity in the RRD: Some Factual Evidence

At first glimpse, the manufacturing activity in the RRD does not appear to be as much developed as in the rest of the country: while the region counts nearly 20 per cent of the national population and labour force and contributes almost 17 per cent to the GDP, its industrial output amounts to no more than 14 per cent of that of the country (see Table A.4 in Appendix 3). Industry (including construction) as a proportion of GDP represents only some 20 per cent at the regional level versus 28 per cent country-wide. The region's industry growth rate and productivity also appear to be low by national standards (see Table 9.1).

Table 9.1   Some features of the RRD region (seven provinces) in 1992

	Country (1)	RRD Region (2)	% of country (2)/(1)
Population (thousand persons)	69,405	13,547	19.5
Density (persons per square km)	214	1,104	
Labour force (thousand persons)	31,815	6,141	19.3
– Agriculture (%)	(73.0)	(70.0)	
– Industry, incl. construction (%)	(13.4)	(10.2)	
– Services (%)	(13.6)	(19.8)	

GDP at current prices (billion dong)	110,535	19,217	17.4
– Agriculture and forestry (%)	(33.0)	(34.7)	
– Industry, incl. construction (%)	(28.2)	(20.4)	
– Services (%)	(38.8)	(44.9)	
Industrial output (Billion dong at constant 1989 prices)	18,117	2,488	13.7
Industrial output – real growth rate			
– 1986-92 (% p.a.)	7.1	4.5	
– 1990–92 (% p.a.)	11.2	2.5	
Industrial output by worker (Thousand dong at constant 1989 prices)	4,275	3,976	

Source: Computed from data given in 'Policy Orientations for the Development of Industry in the Red River Delta Up to the Year 2010', by the Core Counterpart Team (project VIE/89/034), State Planning Committee, Department of Industry.

Despite this apparently unimpressive picture, the RRD's industry structure reveals some salient features that appear to increase the prospects for the region's further industrialization, as described below.

Evolving structure of the manufacturing activity: RRD vs. the rest of the country

Table 9.2 shows the structure of the manufacturing industry in the RRD versus the rest of the country in 1986 and 1990, 1991 and 1992. The International Standards of Industrial Classification (ISIC) has been adopted to facilitate international comparisons.

Compared to the rest of the country, the RRD's manufacturing sector displays a more dynamic and balanced pattern of industrial development. The region's industry structure is in fact more comparable to that of the economies further advanced in the process of industrialization such as Indonesia and Thailand, with a more balanced pattern between basic, intermediate goods and capital goods industries. The proportion between these three categories (basic goods, intermediate goods and capital goods) is 58/28/14 for Indonesia, versus 54/30/16 for the RRD and 70/22/8 for the rest of the country.

Table 9.2   MVA by main branches of industry: RRD vs. rest of country

Manufacturing branches	RRD (%)				Rest of country (%)			
	1986	1990	1991	1992	1986	1990	1991	1992
Food, beverages and tobacco (ISIC 31)	15.8	17.7	19.5	21.8	31.0	50.1	48.9	49.0
Textiles, wearing apparel and leather (ISIC 32)	26.5	27.3	23.5	20.0	16.2	10.5	10.5	11.0
Wood and wood products, incl. furniture (ISIC 33)	5.2	5.9	6.2	6.7	9.8	4.8	4.6	3.6
Paper and paper products and printing (ISIC 34)	3.0	2.3	2.0	2.5	4.5	3.9	3.5	3.5
Chemicals and chemical, rubber and plastic products (ISIC 35)	10.3	7.2	7.2	8.4	10.2	8.2	9.5	10.2
Non-metallic mineral products (ISIC 36)	13.9	18.1	21.5	21.1	8.4	8.3	8.9	8.9
Metal products, excl. machinery (ISIC 381)	0.4	0.1	0.6	0.3	1.7	2.3	3.0	3.5
Machinery and equipment (ISIC 382/383/384/385)	21.8	17.6	16.5	16.2	14.2	8.9	8.3	7.8
Other manufacturing industries (ISIC 39)	3.1	3.7	3.0	3.0	4.0	3.0	2.8	2.5
Total manufacturing	100.0	100.0	100.0	100.0	100.0	100.0	100.0	100.0

Source: Computed from data given in 'Policy Orientations for the Development of Industry in the Red River Delta Up to the Year 2010', by the Core Counterpart Team (project VIE/89/034), State Planning Committee, Department of Industry.

Five major branches have emerged in the RRD's manufacturing sector: agro-food processing (ISIC 31), textiles and garments (ISIC 32) and non-metallic mineral industries (ISIC 36) ranked on equal terms, each sharing some 20 per cent of MVA in 1992; the mechanical/electrical engineering industries (ISIC 382/383/384/385) came next with around 16 per cent of MVA, followed by the chemical industries (ISIC 35) with some 8 per cent of MVA. The part of basic industries (ISIC 31/32/33/34/39) was stable over time, around 54 per cent of MVA in 1986 and 1992. The share of capital goods industries (ISIC 382/383/ 384/385) has somewhat eroded since 1986, but has remained stable from 1990 through 1992.

On the other hand, the rest of the country's manufacturing structure points to the excessive predominance of basic industries (70 per cent of MVA in 1992) over capital goods industries (only 8 per cent of MVA). More oddly, the part of basic industries seems not to have been reduced over time.

The resource base for industry

The extent of industrialization in the RRD closely depends on the overall economic characteristics of the region, due in particular to the predominance of its linkages with the primary sector. While the region has a relatively large agricultural sector (almost 35 per cent of GDP; see Table A.10), it is at the same time fairly well endowed with a number of mineral resources, some of which are currently exploited for local industrial purposes. High-grade anthracite coal has been mined in Quang Ninh province and mostly used in the power stations at Phat Lai, Uong Bi and Ninh Binh, in the Thai Nguyen steel works, and in the Ha Bac urea factory. Metals are not found in large quantities in the Delta (some iron ore is mined at Cau Bai, copper is found at Yen Cu, antimony at Yen Ve), but non-metallic minerals abound. Among them, limestone, silica and clay are the most commercially important materials found in many areas of the region (Ninh Binh, Nam Ha, Ha Tay, Vinh Phu), and are quarried mostly for local manufacturing, primarily for the cement and building materials industries. Apatite is imported from the northern Lao Cai province for the phosphate fertilizer factories in Hanoi, Vinh Phu and Ninh Binh provinces.

There exists a large hydroelectric potential in the Red River basin. There is a huge excess in generating capacity with the 1,920 MW Hoa Binh hydropower plant. In addition, three large coal-fired thermal plants are located at Pha Lai (440 MW), Ninh Binh (100 MW) and Uong Bi (105 MW).

Industrial capability building

Turning now to the industrialization process in the RRD, another characteristic relates to the investment patterns for industrial development. The RRD has a long tradition in industrial investment, not only in the productive (essentially heavy industry) base, but also in the build-up of an impressive human capital stock (see Table A.11). While this is not the place for discussing past investment policy, the fact is clear that the region has over time accumulated considerable capabilities in the capital goods industries. Just to mention a few: the Institute for Machinery and Industrial Instruments (IMI), founded in 1973 at Ha Noi, is now able to design and manufacture complete equipment for most processing plants, and many civil engineering groups such as the Thang Long Group and the Viet Nam Consultant Corporation for Industrial and Urban Construction are in a position to carry out by themselves all major investment projects (e.g. basic and detailed engineering, construction, equipment procurement, testing and assembly, training, start up).

The increasing share of capital goods in the manufacturing activity is generally viewed as both the cause and the consequence of greater technological capacity in mechanical and electrical engineering. Mechanical engineering skills are regarded as the very foundation of all industrial capabilities, while electrical and electronic engineering skills – which come at a later stage – are also considered, under the current technological revolution, of equal importance for operating practically all modern industry.

Moreover, the region is developing a team spirit *(esprit de corps)* – local people have historically shown a remarkable social cohesiveness and a strong sense of accomplishment – which will enable progress, in the years to come, to exceed previous performances.

Major Industries

This section will focus more specifically on the review of the cement and building materials, chemicals and fertilizers, metallurgy, mechanical engineering, and consumer electronics.

Cement and building materials industries

Due to its geographic and economic situation, the RRD has the most dynamic and developed cement and building materials subsector in the country. The region generates more than one third (40 per cent if the three nearby provinces of Ha Bac, Vinh Phu and Quang Ninh are taken into account) of the national subsector's output. The regional cement and building materials subsector is reported to have grown at 13.3 per cent p.a. (versus 7.7 per cent p.a. for the country) during the 1986–1992 period. The present situation of the subsector in the region is as follows:

Cement: There exist two rotary-kiln plants located at Hai Phong and Hai Hung. The Hai Phong cement plant has an installed capacity of 300,000 t/y, and produces two quality standards (Portland and white) of cement; the equipment (from Romania) consists of four rotary kilns (250 t/day clinker x 4) and uses a wet process. The Hoang Thach plant at Hai Hung has an installed capacity of 1.1 million t/y, and produces Portland cement; the equipment (from F. L. Smidth, Denmark) consists of one rotary kiln (3,100 t/day) and uses the dry process. The production of these two plants has been stable over the last three years, at full capacity utilization.

In addition, there are eight small-scale units in the RRD (plus three in the nearby provinces), designed within the range of 3,000–25,000 t/y capacity and using vertical shaft kilns. Since 1975, such units are totally designed and equipped in the country. The combined capacity of these eleven units is estimated to reach 120,000 t/y. Some have recently been modernized and are reported to operate quite satisfactorily (He Duong, Tien Son, Thanh Ba).

A US$ 283.5 million joint-venture cement project with Taiwan Province of China (capacity of 1.4 million t/y) is currently under implemention, including a clinker plant at Hai Phong and a crushing unit (500,000 t/y) located at Vung Tau (southern Viet Nam).

Cement consumption in the region as well as countrywide is still low (70 kg/head country-wide, 126 kg/head in Ho Chi Minh City and 100 kg/head in Ha Noi, compared to 700 kg/head in Bangkok), but is expected to rise rapidly (at around 20 per cent p.a.). According to the Viet Nam National Union of Cement Plants (UCP) – which controls the four national cement factories of Hai Phong, Hoang Thach, Ha Tien (1.3 million t/y) and Bim Son (1.2 million t/y) – the national market is estimated at around 6.5–7 million tonnes in 1995 and forecast to reach 12 million tonnes in 2000. There is a plan to expand the capacity of Hoang Thach plant by 1.2 t/y (implementation scheduled in 1993–1995), of Bim Son plant by 0.6 million t/y (implementation scheduled in 1994–1995) and of Hai Phong plant by 1.2 million tonnes (implementation scheduled in 1995–98).

Other building materials: The RRD concentrates a large number of small- to medium-scale factories producing a vast range of building materials such as bricks, tiles, construction stones, fibro-cement blocks/tiles, glass, inflammable materials, etc. Development opportunities abound in this subsector as the region is rich in non-metallic mineral resources. For example, a US$ 118 million joint-venture project for a float glass production plant (capacity of 28 million square metres/year) in Ha Bac province is currently under consideration, with the involvement of the Viet Nam Construction Glass and Ceramics Corporation (CGCC) and the two Japanese companies, Nippon Sheet Glass and Tomen (*Viet Nam News*, 31 December 1994).

Chemical and fertilizer industries

Due to past government investment policy, the RRD virtually concentrates all the productive capacity in the fertilizer industry. There are five State-owned fertilizer plants: the Lam Thao single superphosphate (SSP) factory in Vinh Phu province, two thermophosphate units at Van Dien (Ha Noi) and Ninh Binh, and the Ha Bac urea plant (see Table 9.3).

The SSP plant has an installed capacity of 500,000 t/y (in 1960) and there is a plan to increase this capacity by an additional 250,000 tonnes. There is also a plan to construct a tri-superphosphate (TSP) plant with a capacity of 250,000 t/y, but no confirmed source of finance has been identified yet.

It is also planned to increase the production capacity of the two thermophosphate units at Van Dien and Ninh Binh to 100,000 t/y from their current capacity of around 40,000 t/y.

The Ha Bac urea plant has an installed capacity of 100,000 t/y (1978) and is operating at full capacity. There is no firm plan to increase the production of nitrogen fertilizer in the region, but it was thought that the discovery of off-shore natural gas in southern Viet Nam could lead to the consideration for a plant using this feedstock to produce ammonia for the manufacture of urea fertilizer.

The chemical industry in the region consists mainly in the production of caustic soda, soap and detergents, batteries, paints, tubes and tyres for bicycles, soldering sticks, and pyrites ores.

By international standards, the overall chemical productive base in the RRD looks tiny and technologically obsolete. The existing factories were mostly established in the 1960s, some with technical assistance from China, but locally designed and equipped. Although some technical improvements have been realized over the years, these factories are considered antiquated. According to the Core Counterpart Team, the scrap value of the existing productive facilities for the whole subsector in the region would not exceed US$ 70 million. And experts in the chemical industry reckon that to develop the caustic soda industry for example, it would be more rational to envisage the development of a completely new project rather than endeavouring to rehabilitate existing capacities.

Table 9.3   Capacity of main chemical and fertilizer plants in the RRD

Products	Capacity Actual (projected)	Capacity utilization in 1993 (per cent)	Percentage share in national capacity	Factory
Single superphosphate (SSP)	500,000 t/y (+250,000 t/y)	85	100	Lam Thao Supe
Thermophosphate (FMP)	80,000 t/y	60	100	Van Dien Phan Lan, Ninh Binh Phan Lan
Trisuperphosphate (TSP)	Nil (250,000 t/y)			
Urea	100,000 t/y	100	100	Ha Bac Phan Dam
Caustic soda	6,000 t/y	60	25	Viet Tri Chemicals
Tubes/tyres for bicycles	5 million units	90	40	Cao Su Ha Noi, Cao Su Hai Phong, Cao Su Thai Binh
Detergents	25,000 t/y	80	25	Xa Phong Ha Noi, Viet Tri Chemicals, Song Cam Chem., Thai Hoa Coop., Duc Giang Chemicals

Table 9.3   (continued)

Products	Capacity Actual (projected)	Capacity utilization in 1993 (per cent)	Percentage share in national capacity	Factory
Standard batteries	60 million units	80	50	Van Dien Battery
Rechargeable batteries	120,000 units	50	40	Vinh Phu Ac Qui, Hai Phong Ac Qui
Paints	6,000 t/y	60	40	Son Tong Hop HN, Son Hai Phong
Soldering sticks	4,000 t/y	30	60	Que Han Thuong Tin
Pyrites ores	100,000 t/y	83	100	Giap Lai, Ba Trai

Source: *Orientations for the Development of the Chemical Industry in the Red River Delta up to Year 2010*, prepared by the Vietnamese Core Counterpart Team (VIE/89/034).

Metallurgy

The country's iron and steel industry is dominated by the Viet Nam Steel Corporation (VSC), which operates five State-owned enterprises: the Thai Nguyen Iron and Steel Complex located in Bac Thai province (northwest of the RRD), and four steel works in the south constituting the Southern Steel Union (SSU).

The Thai Nguyen Complex is an old-aged integrated mill comprising a pig iron making unit, a steel making unit, rolling mills, a coking plant, a refractory brick plant and a ferro-alloy processing plant. Although the complex was originally (1960) designed with a capacity of 130,000 t/y, the present capacity is rated at only 85,000 t/y due to old and obsolete equipment. The complex produces wire rods, steel bars, I-beams, angles and rail.

The SSU operates four steel works using scraps as raw materials to electric arc furnaces to produce steel ingots; three of them are integrated with rolling facilities to provide wire rods and steel bars. These plants are also more than 15 years old, and their present production capacity is 65,000 t/y.

These five factories represent some 150,000 t/y, which accounts for about 80 per cent of the steel production capacity of the country. According to the VSC, the national demand is estimated to be around 700,000 tonnes in 1995 (about 9 kg/head) and to reach 1 million tonnes by the year 2000. It is planned to increase the domestic steel production for construction materials with a target of 300,000 tonnes in 1995 and 500,000–600,000 tonnes in the year 2000, while the requirements for other items of steel products are met by imports.

In the RRD, metal fabricating has not been developed, except for the foundry industry. It is only very recently that the region has tried to cope with its own needs by establishing a certain number of mini steel works, most of which have been realized with minimum investment through self-design and locally-made equipment. They include:

- The steel works of *Duyen Hai Mechanical Engineering Factory* was established in 1992 (investment: US$ 1.3 million). The mill comprises an electric arc furnace (using scrap as raw material) and a self-made rolling unit of 17,000 t/y to produce round bars and steel coil.
- The *Hai Phong rolling mill* (a joint venture between TISCO and the Hai Phong authorities) started its operation in 1993. The mill has a capacity of 8,000 t/y, and was totally designed and equipped by TISCO, main products are: bars (10–12 mm diameter).
- The steel works of the *Tools n.1 Factory* (Ha Noi) comprises two separate units (total investment US$ 700,000), each equipped with electric arc furnace and rolling facility. The first unit (3,000 t/y) was put into operation in 1992 and the second (5,000 t/y) in 1994; main products are wire rods (6–8 mm diameter).
- The steel works of *Ninh Binh Mechanical Engineering Factory* (total investment: US$ 200,000) started to operate in 1992. The mill comprises an electric arc furnace and a small rolling unit of 3,000 t/y; main products are wire rods (6–8 mm diameter).
- The *Dong Anh Steel Works* (a joint venture between several local mechanical engineering factories) was self-designed and equipped (total investment US$ 700,000). It has a capacity of 8,000 t/y; main products are wire rods (6–8 mm diameter).

Due to the lack of modern technologies, these steel works operate at low levels of economic efficiency (e.g. electricity consumption per tonne of steel produced is reported to be 800–1,000 kWh, while it is only 300–500 kWh by international standards), and the output quality is uneven and substandard.

The region could actively seek joint ventures with foreign capital, aimed at establishing one or two new steel rolling mills (100,000–200,000 t/y), fitted with the latest technological developments. This would reinforce the region's technological capabilities in this subsector. As a positive step in this direction, it is worth mentioning a US$ 9.3 million joint-venture project (between VSC and the Republic of Korea for a steel pipe plant (capacity of 30,000 t/y), which is currently under construction at Hai Phong and expected to go into production in early 1995.

Mechanical/electrical engineering industries
The RRD has a privileged position in the mechanical/electrical engineering activities. Most of the important engineering industries are located in the region, which numbers the country's highest proportion of engineers and technicians. Over the years, the region has established the fundamental production base and structure, and it has built up a considerable human capital stock with good knowledge and skills of mechanical operations. The fundamental capability and experience of its engineers and technicians are relatively high as compared to neighbouring countries, although they lack knowledge of modern technologies.

Mechanical and electrical engineering capabilities in the RRD are considerable. Just to mention a few areas as an illustration:

- The *mechanical engineering* industries now manufacture a wide range of conventional machine tools (e.g. rice threshing machines, rice mills), cutting tools (e.g. twist drills, taps), process equipment (e.g. raw-silk processing, sugar processing, coffee and rubber processing, beer and beverage processing, feed mills), measuring instruments (e.g. sliding callipers, micrometers), hand-tools, spare parts and fasteners, insecticide pumps, water pumps, and centrifugal and other special pumps in use in chemical industries. They are able to design and manufacture a large variety of process equipment for industrial plants (e.g. cement plant from 20,000 t/y to 90,000 t/y).

* The *engine fabricating* industries produce a variety of diesel and gasoline engines, agricultural machines (e.g. Lotus 12 CV tractors) and engine/automobile spare parts. Export capabilities for Vietnamese engineering products are also increasing (the 3 January 1995 issue of *Viet Nam News* reports an increase in engine exports: the Viet Nam Engine Factory n.2 (Vinappro) exported about 2,000 D6 (6hp) diesel engines to China (Taiwan Province), Indonesia and Malaysia throughout 1994, a threefold increase since 1993).

* The *electrical engineering* industries produce electric motors (0.6–100 kW), transformers (50–16,000 kVA, voltage 6.3–100 kV), cables, wires, electrical measuring devices and electrical appliances; they are able to manufacture all cooling and refrigerating equipment, notably for food-processing and beverage industries.

With the availability of such capabilities, this industrial subsector in the region has a high potential for further development. Restructuring of the existing factories to take full advantage of horizontal and vertical linkages (for the moment, these units seem to operate all steps of the processes on a self-reliance basis, including casting, forging, stamping and machining) are, however, needed to increase the economic efficiency. Further participation in large-scale investment projects would also be of great importance.

Electronic and informatic industries
This subsector is still at an infant stage, but is growing rapidly. Two government organizations are involved in the development of the industry: *(a)* the Viet Nam Electronics and Informatics Corporation (VEI) and *(b)* the Institute of Electronics and Informatics (IEI).

VEI runs 12 State-owned enterprises, four of which are located in Hanoi. For the moment, these enterprises are essentially involved in complete knocked-down assembly of limited items of microcomputers, television sets and radio-cassette recorders and/or repairing and maintenance services of computers and other electronic appliances. The Corporation emphasizes the need for intensive development of the subsector to substitute imports, particularly by producing materials/

components from locally available raw materials such as ferrite rare earth magnets, electronic ceramics, etc. In a second stage, this subsector could provide a base for export production.

The main task of IEI is to support the scientific and technological development of the industry. Two industrial parks are currently under construction in Ha Noi for the development of high-tech enterprises: the Sai Dong electronic industrial park (covering at present 50 ha, but which could be expanded to 80 ha) was achieved in 1994, and the Soc Son park is still under construction.

Industrial Organization

State-owned enterprises

The realm of SOEs in 1989 spanned over some 12,000 enterprises in various sectors of economic activity, but mostly under the purview of the ministry of defence and the ministry of agriculture and food industry. A major reform introduced in 1989–1990 imposed on SOEs new regulations to increase their exposure to competitive pressures and harden their budget constraints by suspending most of the government transfers they hitherto enjoyed. The reform furthermore requested SOEs to restructure and re-register after compliance with market-like criteria such as minimum legal capital, financial soundness supported by a proper accounting system and an organizational plan. Two thousand companies that did not meet the requirements were liquidated, while an additional 3,000 were merged to take advantage of economies of scale.

The reforms fell short, however, of a full corporatization process inasmuch as SOEs were not allowed to be formally incorporated as commercial entities under the December 1990 Company Law, which does not provide for single-owner (i.e., the State) firms. SOEs therefore remain legally and technically the responsibility of their line ministry which until now assumes ownership, control and management.

The merging of SOEs seems rather at odds with the widespread tendency amongst other transition economies to dismantle State monopolies. It leads to stronger market concentration, deters new entrants, and, by creating complex superstructures, makes even more difficult the assessment of the actual profitability of the enterprise. Moreover, that line ministries should retain the sole responsibility for SOE governance, blurs the accountability of management and decision-making, and raises potential conflicts of interest when the same line ministries are called to endorse new investments in their field.

Nevertheless, the reforms succeeded in restructuring the SOE sector and improving its performance. By late 1993, the total number of SOEs had decreased to 7,000, while the number of industrial SOEs had reduced from 3,020 to 2,270 over the same period. Total employment in the industrial sector amounted to 3.5 million workers in 1992, of which SOEs represented one fifth (Tables A.1 and A.9). In terms of manufacturing output, SOEs accounted the same year for 60 per cent of the total (Table A.3), mostly under the supervision of the local states (Table A.5).

The size of industrial SOEs is typically in the 1–500 employee bracket (Tables A.6 and A.7). They are prominent in the energy sector, chemicals and construction materials, while they occupy a somewhat less dominant position in light industries such as food processing and textiles (Table A.3). Despite the loss of their traditional CMEA markets, their growth has been steadily strong in the 1990s, and has constantly outpaced non-State manufacturing activities over the same period (Table A.2). Yet output growth figures of industrial SOEs must be interpreted cautiously, as they include electricity and oil where large investments recently came into operation, and because they also reflect the fact that SOEs benefited from generous public investment flows in general. But they do, none the less, reveal a more positive trend, i.e., a general diversification of product lines away from the excessive reliance on heavy manufactures to include now consumer goods such as detergents, electric fans, household cables and bicycle parts.

Non-State enterprises

Non-State enterprises fall under three categories: the cooperatives, the private enterprises – in the form of sole proprietorship, limited liability, or shareholding companies – and the private household enterprises – mostly family crafts. A decree by the Politburo in April 1988 established the household rather than the cooperative as the basic productive unit and triggered a massive outflow of workers from the cooperatives to newly established private household businesses (Table A.5).

In 1992, the non-State enterprises employed four fifths of the total workers in the industrial sector, and contributed 40 per cent of the total manufacturing output. They are found in food processing, textiles, construction materials and wood processing where they are far stronger than their SOE counterparts (Table A.3).

With a dwindling population of cooperatives and household enterprises accounting for employment much more than for value-added, the growth of the non-State sector lies on private industries which have behaved remarkably well since the introduction of 'Doi Moi'. Yearly growth rates have been impressive since 1987 (Table A.2) in spite of modest investments (Table A.8), indicating a natural drive to labour-intensive processes. The trend is encouraging: in 1993, the exports from the private industrial sector recorded a twofold increase over the 1992 figure. However, if the private industries sector is to further expand and penetrate international markets, it must gradually move to more sophisticated technologies, and will require in the process more substantial investment flows. The Government is well aware of these prospects, and has recently offered attractive incentives aimed at mobilizing domestic savings to feed private investment.

10. Prospects for Manufacturing Growth in the Red River Delta: Elements of Strategic Planning

Conceptual Issues

As for any programming exercise, the process of strategic planning starts from three elements:

- An assessment of the initial situation (or 'state', in decision theory);
- A characterization of the target situation (objectives, or 'consequences');
- An identification of the prevailing constraints.

Applied to the manufacturing sector in the Red River Delta region, it builds on:

- A survey of the relevant resources in the region, including natural endowments, physical infrastructure, human resources and the existing industrial capacities (Chapter 9);
- A delineation of the development objectives for the country and for the region, as spelled out by the public authorities. This essential component is treated below; it clearly involves judgements of value, as alternative industrialization patterns are likely to generate different socio-economic impacts;
- A summary of the constraints, at both the overall and the business levels, hindering manufacturing growth.

The planning process consists of mapping out the most appropriate scenario to drive the economy or the sector from the present to the desired situation, given the constraints. In a command economy, the planning process translates into a centralized allocation of available resources to productive activities, aimed at quantitative output targets. An industrial 'plan' in this context typically features a stocktaking of physical resources, demand forecasts and a public investment programme to lay out the required capacities to service future needs. Responsibility for the implementation of the plan rests exclusively with the centre or the public authority.

A market economy on the contrary displays a multitude of agents, firms and consumers that interact on a daily basis and eventually shape the economy. They pursue specific agendas, responding to decentralized, market signals, and distribute resources accordingly. The process of strategic planning is therefore fundamentally different, and probably far more complex, in that it must apprehend the economic rationale underlying production and consumption patterns, and discern areas where market forces alone may fail to deliver long-term growth and sustainable social development. The planner, i.e., the Government, is but one player among others in the complex, multi-agent decision-making process that drives the industrialization of the country. Thus it must furthermore identify strategic variables where it can leverage the strongest beneficial impact on the overall outcome, and deploy to that end the instruments at its disposal (the 'acts', in decision theory, further detailed in Chapter 11).

In an open economy turning increasingly global, manufacturers compete in the international scene to enlarge their market share, increase their profits or simply stay in business. They are more likely to succeed if their processes are firmly rooted in actual comparative advantages. Yet the essence of comparative advantages can be subject to rapid changes, and their identification may furthermore be blurred by restrictive trade policies and other interferences with natural market mechanisms. The strategy of the Government must therefore seek a fuller realization and the further diversification of comparative advantages in manufacturing.

Development Objectives of the Government for the Red River Delta

Country-wide objectives of industrialization
With the recent attainment of food self-sufficiency (Viet Nam has become a net exporter of rice), and encouraged by a buoyant inflow of

foreign capital, the Government has decisively shifted its emphasis towards industrialization as a vector of growth. The Seventh Plenum of the Central Committee, held 25–30 July 1994, mapped out a comprehensive industrialization policy framework aimed at increasing the industry's contribution to GDP to 30 per cent by the end of the decade.

Led by the party general secretary, the Plenum outlined the main axes of the new industrialization strategy, featuring:

- A shift from heavy to light industry and labour-intensive manufacturing, to reflect the country's large endowments in labour and scarcity of land and capital. Agro-processing, machinery, electronics and consumer goods in general were explicitly mentioned by the general secretary as target industries in the future;
- An export bias, as a way to accelerating job creation, income generation and capital formation;
- A gradual process of import substitution;
- A reform of the State business sector, and a stronger support to private sector development;
- Emphasis on improving the quality and upgrading the technology to bring Viet Nam at par with international standards.

In terms of economic growth the Government's target is to double the per capita GDP during the period 1991–2000. Other interrelated key objectives highlighted in the Government's report to the Consultative Groups Meeting in November 1994 were:

- Macroeconomic stability with strong and sustainable growth;
- Continuing structural change, with the share of industry and services expected to increase and that of agriculture to decline. The growth rate of industry is expected to be 1.5 times that of total GDP. Accordingly, its share of total GDP is expected to grow from 21 per cent to 28–30 per cent between 1993 and 2000;
- Development of key industries where Vietnam has a comparative advantage so as to develop a more dynamic and efficient industrial sector;
- The promotion of appropriate technology to increase productivity and product quality;

- The development of the infrastructure needed to support commercial investments;
- Development of the rural economy; through improvements in productivity of agriculture, forestry and fishery production the modernization of agriculture and the development of rural industry will be critical to improving living standards of rural communities;
- Special attention to the needs of the isolated mountainous and coastal communities;
- Development of human resources and institutions critical to achieving and sustaining real development. This includes training and education, improvement in health services, the development of social and economic infrastructure, improved financial institutions to mobilize and allocate savings, development of legal institutions and improved public administration (including development planning).

The Red River Delta

There are no official objectives specific to the industrial development of the RRD region; increased prosperity in the Delta is seen basically as a means of contributing to the attainment of national growth targets while alleviating regional disbalances across the country. However, staff from the Ministry of Science, Technology and Environment working in the project's Core Counterpart Team on Industry have translated countrywide guidelines set out by the Party, into the practical requirements they entail for the industrialization process in the region.

Thus the inferred regional objectives become:

- The share of industry in GDP growing from 20 per cent (1992) to 26 per cent in 2000 and 32 per cent in 2010;
- An annual industry growth rate of 12 per cent through the end of the decade.

MOSTE proposes to this end a series of industrial development directions including, *inter alia*:

- A fuller exploitation of the region's natural and human resources;
- A strong export bias;

- A structural adjustment of manufacturing patterns to better service the domestic market in the RRD region in particular, but also in the whole country;
- High-skill and clean industries in Hanoi;
- The modernization of existing facilities and infrastructures;
- A focus on agro-based industries and handicrafts.

The Constraints

Macroeconomic and institutional constraints

These constraints were elaborated upon in Chapter 8. For the sake of convenience they are summarized here, by order of their occurrence in the text:

- The risk of a devaluation, even of a sliding type;
- Shallow financial depth; an inverted interest rate structure and a tax schedule on banking operations that discourages long-term lending;
- The multiplier effect of a turnover tax on businesses and a profit tax that allows no deduction for reinvestment;
- The multiplicity of tariff rates with cascading effect;
- Loopholes in the legal apparatus, hence possible misinterpretations and arbitrary decisions by the authorities;
- Cumbersome regulations; slow procedures that lack transparency;
- Absence of effective institutional support to private ventures.

Business constraints

Apart from general hindrances in the overall environment, a number of obstacles at business level are reported by the – existing or would-be – entrepreneurs themselves:

- Low income per capita in Viet Nam and thus, a limited domestic market in spite of the population size;
- Weak infrastructure;
- Bureaucratic hurdles;
- Rising business costs i.e. soaring land prices, commercial and residential rents, hotel and taxi fares, telecommunication costs;
- Land use and land expropriation problems;
- Difficulties in indentifying the right joint-venture partner.

Tentative Assessment of Comparative Advantages in Manufacturing

The growing complexity of the economic activity and its accelerated globalization altered over time the very nature of comparative advantages, the dynamics of which have become increasingly remote from the availability of natural resources or the relative abundance of production factors. Comparative advantages today feed on a subtle interaction of human resources, capital and knowledge that together allow for the steady accumulation of technological capabilities and the ability to reproduce, improve or create sophisticated manufacturing processes. Strengthening and developing such capabilities is a protracted process where the State can play a prominent role, as clearly demonstrated in neighbouring South-East Asian countries.

There are basically two ways of assessing comparative advantages. The first approach elicits these from the analysis of external trade flows, where a surge in exports for a given manufacture reveals the strengthening of an underlying comparative advantage. It is said *ex post* because it does not foresee the emergence of comparative advantages: it barely highlights the fact. Its *ex ante* variant builds on a careful survey of factor costs in a given country, as compared to the same analysis, systematically carried in competing countries. Major discrepancies of relative factor costs across countries then indicate comparative advantages.

Both approaches, particularly the second one, are time consuming. When applied to a subset of the economy such as the Red River Delta Region of Viet Nam, they furthermore cannot rely on generally published statistics, usually aggregated at the national level. An attempt is however made below to delineate revealed comparative advantages, while a market proxy provides a measure of prior advantages. The trends depicted in Figures 10.1 and 10.2 are based on data provided in Tables A.12 and A.13 in the Annex.

Revealed comparative advantages

As Viet Nam is still characterized by a large SOE sector, it is difficult to infer comparative advantages from the evolution of trade patterns in the RRD region. Indeed manufacturing output and trade in a particular region can be heavily promoted by the Government for a variety of reasons beyond strict economic rationale. Furthermore as foreign trade statistics do not disaggregate at the region's level, value-added figures have been utilized instead.

To have an appreciation of what constitutes the RRD's comparative advantages, we rely on Figure 10.1, which compares the structure of the manufacturing sector in the RRD versus the rest of the country, in terms of the degree of complexity involved in manufacturing activities. Figure 10.1 also shows the evolution of the manufacturing structure between 1986 and 1992.

Figure 10.1   *Structural composition of manufacturing value-added: RRD vs. rest of country*

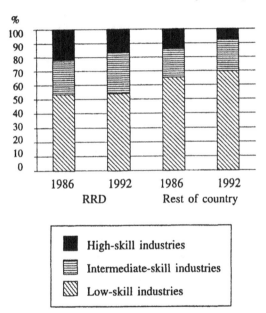

Three categories of industries appear in the bar chart, according to a typical structure of wage levels: low-skilled (ISIC 31/32/33/34/39), intermediate-skilled (ISIC 35/36) and high-skilled (ISIC 38) industries. The breakdown highlights striking differences: the RRD manufacturing sector has kept its part of intermediate and high-skilled industries at around 45 per cent of MVA between 1986 and 1992, while this already smaller part in the national manufacturing sector has been further reduced from 37 per cent to 33 per cent during the same period.

Limited availability of data does not allow for more elaborate treatment at this stage. This cursory analysis emphasizes however that the

RRD shows the basic fundamentals required to move towards more sophisticated manufacturing activities.

This measure confirms the widespread recognition that the RRD has a relatively strong position in two distinct areas: the building materials branch and the mechanical/electrical engineering industries, which need to be developed and reinforced to spearhead the region's further industrialization. To develop these two areas, the region can readily build on its human capital stock.

Perceived comparative advantages

For all the economic theory and reasoning, a strong industrialization process will ultimately result from investment decisions and business plans, drawn by a large number of domestic and foreign entrepreneurs. Before committing their own resources to risky, long-term ventures, potential investors will first carry out a detailed analysis to spot countries showing an attractive – expected – return for a given manufacturing segment. They are the best judges to balance factor costs, risks and other particulars in different countries, before ultimately picking the one that best suits their needs.

Therefore the structure, in terms of magnitude and sectoral distribution, of foreign capital inflows conveys valuable information on the nature of comparative advantages. An obvious example, if not an information breakthrough, stems from the impressive manufacturing growth recorded in 1993 at the cost of a relatively low ICOR, by the standards of low-income developing countries. It underpins a broad trend towards labour-intensive industries and the exploitation of Viet Nam's comparative advantage in cheap labour.

As investments – particularly at the stage of commitments only – are easily a few years ahead of actual production, the approach by investment figures takes a lead over the alternative based on trade data. Of course, unlike trade statistics, investment data may be misleading as they certainly encompass projects that will eventually fail for a number of reasons, including a wrong assessment of comparative advantages. Furthermore, the approach is not immune to the distortions embedded in the prevailing policies: for instance a number of car manufacturers have expressed interest in operating in the country, probably attracted by the huge effective protection this industry enjoys in the domestic market. Yet this fact should not introduce in the analysis a systematic bias, as *(a)* the domestic market remains limited in purchasing power terms, and *(b)* the strived-for admission into the ASEAN group[1] will certainly entail a general reduction of the tariff structure, and one may reasonably assume that this risk factor has been duly incorporated in the investment decision.

Finally, a correction should ideally be introduced to account for varying capital intensity across manufacturing subsectors; in doing so, the figures would be more readily comparable across subsectors as they would convey a standardized information in terms of value-added prospects. However, what matters here is primarily a survey of 'RRD vs. rest of country' FDI patterns, and we may reasonably assume therefore that capital-labour ratios remain invariant across the two cases.

Figure 10.2 is based on records of all investment proposals between early 1988 and 31 December 1993, maintained by SCCI. In cases where the original investment licence was revoked by the end of 1993, the project is withdrawn from the list.

Figure 10.2   Structural composition of FDI flows in manufacturing: RRD vs. rest of country

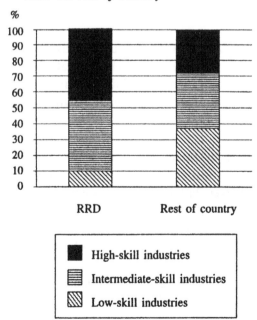

Note: Total value of licensed projects, 1988–1992, see Table A.13, p. 190.

Disaggregate data have been compiled at ISIC two-digit level, from 393 project proposals in the whole of Viet Nam (of which 57 are in the RRD) amounting to US$ 2,659 million (of which US$ 675 million in the RRD). While the region's share in dollar terms is at par with its share of the population, it attracts a much smaller number of projects, thus indicating on the part of potential investors a capital-intensive bias in the Red River Delta.

For the clarity of the figure, the statistics are aggregated, as in the previous section, into low-, intermediate- and high-skill industries. Figure 10.2 demonstrates the strong appeal of the region, viewed from a foreign investor's angle, for capital goods and electronics manufacturing and highlights a strong comparative advantage – at least *vis-à-vis* the rest of the country – in high-skill industries. This is explained by the presence of the capital city and thus better-than-average infrastructure and education facilities, and by a somewhat higher concentration of a skilled workforce trained in the local SOEs.

Key Strategic Options

The strategy for increased industrialization in the Red River Delta must therefore revolve around:

*   The fuller realization of existing comparative advantages;
*   The expansion of the region's technological capabilities, allowing for a diversification of traditional comparative advantages and thus for a stronger resilience to volatile competitive pressures.

It will materialize by means of a progressive restructuring of the manufacturing sector, as it stands now, to exploit or develop dynamic comparative advantages. In this respect, it is useful to disaggregate the manufacturing sector into three segments in terms of their potential concurrence to the effective implementation of the strategy and, ultimately, to the achievement of its targets as follows:

*   The *export-oriented segment* can contribute significantly to both strategic goals. As it is backed to a large extent by foreign capital, it is implicitly shaped by the exploitation of underlying comparative advantages; facing international competitors, its growth

prospects will be determined by its capacity to upgrade its productivity and processes, to adjust to changing competitive pressures and to strengthen its technological capabilities. At present, exports of manufactures remain modest and originate essentially from basic industries such as textile and food processing, but these activities are poised for strong growth in the RRD region if investment pledges in this field are encouraged to materialize. Investment prospects in capital goods in the region have received a tremendous boost in 1993, with a US$ 170 million offer to set up a large television set production plant in Hanoi. This carries a positive message in terms of the perceived comparative advantages of the region, and suggests confidence in its actual capacity to eventually graduate into more sophisticated manufacturing lines.

- The *inward-bound segment* meets the objective of a better exploitation of existing assets, but in view of prevailing protection rates and official plans for further non-tariff barriers, it is unlikely to promote the sustained accumulation of world-class technological skills. However, giant investment commitments in the cement industry would generate sizeable employment and value-added and propel the region's growth.

- The *SOE segment* cannot be expected to concur much to the successful implementation of the strategy; in spite of the bold reforms it went through in the beginning of the decade, it still operates in a sheltered economic space as it continues to benefit from strong, if indirect, government backing. Thus it fails to efficiently exploit the region's present advantages, let alone to develop new capabilities. Traditionally oriented towards heavy industries, it has cushioned surprisingly well the loss of its former CMEA markets, and has shown positive signs of adapting to its new situation by diversifying into consumer goods. It provides a large proportion of the region's manufacturing employment, and a stronger than average contribution to its growth. Nevertheless, it hinders private sector growth in two respects: first, because it absorbs an undue share of the domestic investment potential and second, because it diverts a significant proportion of joint-venture solicitations by foreign partners by virtue of its appreciable links to public authorities. As the business environment improves in future years, it should progressively recede to give room to an expanding private entrepreneurship, better able to detect and take advantage of emerging opportunities.

The strategy lies in a comprehensive growth scenario for each one of the three segments of the manufacturing sector in the RRD region. Its effective implementation calls for a balanced package of reforms and incentives, as outlined in the next chapter.

Note

1. Granted in July 1995.

11. Proposals for a Programme of Action

General Considerations

The expansion of the manufacturing sector in the Red River Delta along the lines of the key strategic options will be driven to a large extent by private sector initiatives. The Government must, however, encourage and support industrialization endeavours by a comprehensive deployment of its financial resources and policy influence.

Different instruments are indeed available to the State; for the sake of presentation, they are grouped here into long-, medium- and short-term actions with reference not to the time horizon of their practical effectiveness, but to their maturity and to the time-lag from their implementation to the supply response they are designed to foster.

Long-term actions are mostly in terms of a public investment programme, which must be sharply focused to defuse the potentially dangerous budget tensions. They must essentially be aimed at:

- Improving the physical infrastructure in roads, utilities and communications facilities: A number of studies in this field have been produced lately, with emphasis for some of them on dedicated areas for manufacturing activities such as industrial estates and export processing zones in the Hanoi-Haiphong-Cai Lan triangle. The Red River Delta Master Plan mostly concentrates on these aspects. Worth mentioning here is the recent package of incentives heavily promoted by the Government in an attempt to attract BOT projects and thus afford the development of infrastructures without further burdening the budget.
- Building human resources: In spite of the high literacy rate recorded in Viet Nam, there are growing concerns in the country that human resource development may suffer the setback of

budget restrictions. Furthermore, the proportion of university graduates and technicians remains low by ASEAN standards, although the RRD region seems to fare better in this respect, thanks to the higher concentration of schools and colleges around the capital.

Direct public investment in the productive industry should be avoided to save scarce resources, but also to avert its adverse crowding-out effect with private businesses, at a time when the Government must on the contrary encourage the mobilization of private finance through the growth of domestic savings and investment flows.

Medium-term actions address the sphere of industrial organization. They are meant to provide effective support to a more integrated network of manufacturing enterprises and related services in the region, and include:

- The creation or reconversion of industry-oriented institutions to cater to the needs of a growing population of private, often small-scale, businesses. Of paramount importance in this respect is a redefinition of the banking industry which should abandon its present biases in favour of the SOEs sector, and against long-term lending to the private sector.
- The further reduction of the influence of the industrial SOE sector, which in various ways continues to inhibit private initiatives; although they have been brought by the 1990 reforms to face a binding budget constraint like any other enterprise, they still benefit from unfair competitive practices, such as favourable access to credit and privileged links to the policy makers. Full corporatization should be implemented, and, as soon as warranted by the growing stock of private capital, non-strategic SOEs should be privatized either as a whole, or through the sale of viable spin-offs. A UNDP-funded, World Bank-executed project is currently analysing alternative scenarios.
- Finally, a gradual adjustment of the Government itself to its new role of facilitating private sector development and monitoring possible obstacles to a fair, competitive game. As the direct responsibility of the line ministries to run public enterprises will diminish in the future, the Government would do well in recycling idle capacities to prevent deviant behaviours that will

inevitably arise to dodge competitive pressures, and on the contrary to encourage compliance with market forces. The Government must develop ties with the business community to better apprehend its needs, aspirations and constraints. Considerable capacity-building will be required in this area, ranging from a stream-lining of the technical ministries in line with the new range of services they are expected to deliver in the future, to a progressive decentralization of public authority from the capital to the provinces.

As for the *short-term measures,* they relate primarily to the careful use of policy instruments to stimulate manufacturing growth. Empirical evidence in Viet Nam suggests indeed that these are high-power management tools, in the sense that they can trigger an extremely rapid, and some times sweeping, supply response. They are of two orders:

- Further deregulation, or the pursuit of a business-friendly policy environment, through increased transparency of the legal framework and appropriate reforms of the tariffs, tax regime and structure of interest rates, to name but a few. These aspects were discussed in earlier chapters.
- A considerable uplifting of the regulatory apparatus and procedures that are seen as major hindrances to private entrepreneurship. The administration must develop market-like performance criteria if it is to improve its productivity and deliver quality services with reasonable delays. This aspect has also been treated in previous chapters.

Specific Considerations for the Industrialization of the Red River Delta

Background: a dual pattern of development in the RRD
Over-populated and much less endowed in land and agricultural resources than the Mekong Delta, the RRD needs to diversify its economy and move beyond agriculture for development purposes. Agriculture still accounts for nearly 35 per cent of the gross regional product and employs more than 70 per cent of the labour force. The average farmholding is 0.3 ha (hardly viable in subsistence terms), and there

are few prospects for further expanding the cultivated area or increasing cropping intensities beyond present levels. Therefore, the Government is placing a major thrust on the need to entice people away from such marginal holdings through the development of industry and services in the region.

Industrial development tends to be concentrated in the region's upper boundary, along the main Viettri-Hanoi-Haiphong axis and to some locations in Quang Ninh province, where natural advantages (such as energy, raw materials, port sites) and acquired benefits (such as transport, trade and financial services) for industrial production and trade development are found. The rest of the RRD remains essentially agricultural, with an underdeveloped processing industry. The recent establishment of the Hanoi-Haiphong-Quang Ninh Economic Focal Area – also called the North Triangle Zone (NTZ) – to attract FDI and high-tech joint ventures seems to have exacerbated the phenomenon of twin-track industrialization in the region, between the NTZ and the Delta itself (excluding the NTZ). This is reflected in the recent upsurge of applications for numerous locations of industrial estates in several provincial cities of the Delta. Moreover, recent reforms in the Government's rural development policy and subsequent investments in agriculture, forestry and irrigation seem to have revived the interest for new agricultural processing activities. For example, the biggest province of Hai Hung (2,550 km² of land area, 168,000 ha under cultivation, and 2.6 million population) has a food output well over 1.2 million t/y, but its processing industry is limited to three husking factories with a consolidated capacity of 50,000 t/y, which explains, to some extent, why Hai Hung has not exported rice yet.[1]

Present investment indicators suggest that conditions are being set for strong growth in the construction, transport, industrial and services sectors concentrated in Hanoi, Haiphong, Quang Ninh and the corridors connecting these centres. The direct beneficiaries of this investment will be, in overwhelming proportion, the urban populations of the key development area. While this is consistent with the objective of restructuring the economy, it will lead to substantial adjustment pressures which will dominate development issues of the Delta itself (excluding the NTZ).

Income disparities as indicated in the GRP figures for 1993 between the NTZ (US$ 256/head) and the rest of the RRD (US$ 150/head) are significant, and the threat of aggravating income inequalities and subsequent massive rural migration to the major cities of Hanoi and Haiphong have finally stressed the need for reorienting development strategies towards more balanced growth, especially between rural and urban sectors, and integration of rural with urban development. Reflecting such emerging trends in policy formulation, the project Core Counterpart Team, made up of staff from the State Planning Committee, recommended that prefeasibility studies for establishing *(a)* a region-wide viable network for sustaining the development of agro-industries and handicrafts, and *(b)* regional growth centres, be included in the RRD action programme with a view to assisting the promotion of industries in non-metropolitan areas and developing policy guidelines for the governmental assistance required to that end.

The problem of industrialization of the RRD is by all means complex. There is indeed no single development strategy that would seem appropriate for rapid industrial expansion; instead, a strategy mix would be more likely to generate the best possible results. While a growth strategy, which would entail a strong export orientation, looks adequate for a rapid development of the NTZ (enjoying better factor endowments), a basic needs and resource-based strategy appears more suitable to cope with the development level of the rest of the Delta (excluding the NTZ). This will put emphasis on agro-processing and handicrafts, and the promotion of small-scale industries, and will call for massive institutional and financial support for the development of generally small-scale private entrepreneurship.

Technological development for the high growth segment

Technological development can be viewed as the process of acquiring and deepening technological capabilities to foster economic and industrial development. The RRD appears to count an important stock of scientists and engineers. Over the years, it has demonstrated its industrial capabilities in capital goods manufacturing. It is worth noting that the share of capital goods in MVA normally rises with the level of industrial development: this is viewed both as the cause and the consequence of greater technological capacity in mechanical and electrical engineering. Mechanical engineering skills are regarded as the very foundation of all industrial capabilities. Electrical and electronic engineering skills come at a later stage, but the current technological revolution is making them of equally fundamental importance in operating practically all modern industry.

A country's ability to master technical change is a direct function of the technological capabilities it has accumulated in the past. New or emerging technologies pose quite different challenges from those which led to the acquisition of existing capabilities; the ability to respond to these challenges in turn depends on the capacity to learn, train, adapt and compete. Experience has shown that it is such countries which have demonstrated the greatest national technological capabilities that will continue to cope best with new technologies in the future.

According to Lall,[2] such technological capabilities refer to a wide range of skills needed to perform all the technical functions entailed in setting up, operating, improving, expanding and modernizing all industrial facilities. These skills can be grouped under three broad headings: investment, production and linkages capabilities.

Investment capabilities hint at the skills needed to set up a new industrial project or expand an existing facility. They refer to the particular skills needed before undertaking the investment (e.g., project preparation, identification of site and technology supplier, negotiation for construction and technology transfer), and those needed for carrying out the investment itself (e.g., basic and detailed engineering, construction, equipment procurement, testing and montage, training, start-up). Many of these investment functions are normally not carried out by the manufacturer since advanced types of process design require very specialized capabilities, and even some relatively simple functions like civil engineering require organizational and engineering skills that industrial firms are unlikely to possess. However, in-house capabilities to evaluate what specialized engineering consultants recommend, to negotiate favourable terms for technology transfer, to select and procure the right package of equipment, to participate in process design such that specific needs are met, to understand how the plant operates, and so on, are all essential for successful, economical investment by a firm.[3]

Enos and Park (1987) describe how the Republic of Korea built up such capabilities in petrochemicals by a systematic process of participating in investment functions, and show the benefits achieved in terms of cost and productivity. This ingredient of the Republic of Korea's industrial success – its investment capabilities – has often been understated. Across a broad range of industries, the Republic of Korea has consistently achieved lower investment costs than international norms, and simultaneously built up its mastery of the technologies involved. This capacity dates back to before its export-oriented industrialization strategy, and was partly instrumental in the strategy's success. At the other extreme lies sub-Saharan Africa, where a dramatic lack of local investment capabilities results, in spite of a heavy reliance on foreign contractors, in often delayed, and altogether much costlier, projects than elsewhere. Heavy foreign dependence also means that there is little understanding of the technologies transferred, leading to subsequent high operating costs and poor maintenance.[4]

Production capabilities include what is normally understood by 'technology'. They range from basic skills (e.g., quality control, layout, maintenance, inventory control and implementation of designs) to equipment 'stretching', improvement and innovation. Some capabilities may be developed with a minimal base of formal skills (especially in simple technologies). Others may require fairly high levels of schooling and training, institutional effort and further investments in equipment, consultants or the purchase of technology.[5]

And finally, *linkage capabilities* are the specific skills needed by an enterprise to interact with its external environment. These involve the ability to locate efficient suppliers and set up information-exchange mechanisms that characterize inter-industry transactions. Japanese firms have developed an edge in product innovation in several activities, such as automobiles, by building close linkages with suppliers and subcontractors from the early stages of design to the final stages of production.[6]

The capability-building process requires time and investment and entails a certain risk. Higher levels of capability development and the entry into more complex activities do indeed carry higher risk and cost (for instance, the Malaysian electronic industry until now has put heavy pressure on the national trade balance as a large proportion of its inputs still relies on imports), but they constitute areas of future growth as easy opportunities are progressively used up. There is no predictable nor automatic learning curve along which a country can evolve, since it is the level and effectiveness of investment in capability acquisition that ultimately shape the outcome. These investments are in turn determined by a number of factors including, *inter alia*, the competitive and macroeconomic environment surrounding the firms; the level of development and flexibility of factor markets and industrial support systems; the adequacy of physical infrastructures; the sophistication of the science and technology set-up; and the functioning of various legal, financial, marketing and other institutions on which the market system depends. Each country generates a unique outcome depending upon the interplay of these factors, with government policy playing an important role, positive as well as negative.[7]

As for the Red River Delta, we may anticipate certain development issues, which appear to be of fundamental importance in the capability-building process, especially in this particular phase of graduation to an industrial economy.

First, it is clear that in the years ahead, there will be a sustained inflow of physical capital and investment in the region; several projects will come on stream to sustain industrial development. It is of critical importance that the region consolidate its present base of investment capabilities. Such a strong local base (e.g., an expanding core of engineering consultants) can offer significant benefits. It can considerably lower the capital costs of projects, not just because local engineering skills are usually far cheaper, but also because project execution is quicker. Local investment capabilities also enable better adaptation of process designs, greater use of local equipment and greater diffusion of technology within the country (as a rule of thumb, in the implementation of an industrial project, the consulting and engineering services represent some 10–15 per cent of the total investment cost, construction takes another 25–30 per cent, and the rest (50–60 per cent) accounts for equipment, a substantial share of which can be routed to domestic suppliers provided adequate industrial consulting and civil engineering support can be locally available).

To start with, a small number of high-profile professionals will be selected from different departments such as feasibility studies, architectural and civil engineering, and product and process development and design within SOEs engaged in the construction and engineering industries. This core of professionals will be 'externalized' (pulled out of the enterprises) to form an independent engineering and management consultancy business. The bulk of engineering design activities is normally filled up by draughtsmen, technicians and technical designers for basic and detailed engineering in civil, mechanical, electrical and instrument disciplines. This personnel is normally available in the region and can be trained fairly quickly. The more complex part of the expertise concerns project management (planning, cost and quality control), process engineering, testing and montage, start-up and commissioning capabilities, which may not exist in the region. In this case, international assistance can be sought to compensate such deficiencies in locally available expertise.

A systematic process of committing this core of engineering consultants in all investment projects should be established with the firm support and determination of the Government. At the beginning, local participation in project implementation might be low (e.g., 10 per cent of total investment), but on a rapidly increasing trend. At the end, local participation must form the major component in any project implementation, and the part of foreign expertise could be substantially reduced. This policy must cut across the previous industrial tradition of production self-sufficiency of each enterprise.

The build-up of a viable base to supply the domestic parts and components and equipment industry constitutes the next area for the RRD's technological development. With the emergence of the electronics industry and car assembly operations in the NTZ, priority must be given to the development of a strong parts and components industry in the region. It is only out of parts manufacturing that the assembly sector can grow. A biased processing pattern in favour of final (assembled) products is the natural consequence of neglecting capability generation in small- and medium-scale enterprises (SMEs) while promoting assembly operations.

In the context of the RRD, an efficient supply system of parts and components can be considered of particular importance in terms of its contribution towards a self-sustained industrial development by generating industrial linkages and a higher portion of value-added to be retained in the region. It is also a means for enhancing the technological capabilities of small- and medium-scale enterprises involved in such operations as foundry, forging, metal cutting and machining, mould making, metal components and parts production, heat treatment and surface finishing, non-electrical machinery, electrical and electronic components production. Finally, it provides the opportunity to diversify manufacturing exports towards products of greater technological sophistication.

The Japanese model of industrial production based on several layers of component suppliers is often cited as a model for enhancing competitiveness. The reliance on subcontractors for parts and components is an integral part of the Japanese system of industrial production.

However, such a system of industrial production when applied in Viet Nam would need significant prior improvements, notably in the technological and financial capabilities of SMEs.

The development of a strong domestic supply base requires from the Government a firm commitment in extensive support programmes and a clear technology policy. It is interesting in this respect to see how the Republic of Korea has built up such capabilities by extensive support programmes, one of which is the Technology Support Centre for SMEs. In addition to departments for technology transfer and general technical support services, the facility includes specialized foundry and precision machinery centres. Each one of these departments assists hundreds of SME entrepreneurs every year. The department for technology transfer has extensive contacts with Japan, the United States and several European countries, as well as with multilateral organizations such as UNIDO. The department for technical support services is also involved in research and development on behalf of SMEs, in fields designated as national priorities.

Finally, with regard to strengthening the indigenous technological base, special attention should be given to the technology imports policy. Strategy towards both the degree of reliance on technology imports and the form such imports may take is of great importance for indigenous technological capability development. Technology imports in certain forms are a critical input into the development process, but overdependence on foreign technology, particularly in forms that do not call for local learning of basic technologies, can be damaging to the domestic technological capabilities in the long term. In general, technology imports under the highly packaged form (e.g., direct investment) would be convenient for smaller and less-developed countries. But as size and capabilities increase, the development of national technological capabilities may call for greater local efforts relative to technology imports, and for more technology imports in the form of licensing and capital goods rather than foreign direct investment.[8]

A programme for integrated industrialization in the Delta

As already mentioned, industrial development in the Delta (excluding the NTZ) is still very limited and largely confined to small-scale agro-processing and handicrafts. The present pattern of investment, heavily skewed in favour of the NTZ, is likely to encourage an extremely high rate of urbanization, concentrated in only a few metropolitan centres.

There is a need to guide and attract investment to provincial centres and subcentres and to the rural areas.

In view of these considerations, it is highly recommended that a survey project[9] on integrated industrialization in the Delta (excluding the NTZ) be initiated, with a view to assisting the promotion of industries in non-metropolitan areas and developing policy guidelines for the governmental assistance required to that end. The outcome of the survey is the establishment of pilot projects in various locations in the Delta as an innovative approach for accelerated industrialization in non-metropolitan areas.

Objectives of the survey

The objectives of the survey include:

- To design the basic components and contents of the core activities needed for the implementation of the pilot projects;
- To undertake economic appraisal of individual activities and of the pilot project as a whole;
- To programme other aspects of managerial and administrative requisites for its implementation.

Outline of the survey

In line with the objectives listed above, the survey in the Delta consists of the following parts:

- Identification of economic resources and industrial structure in each province;
- Identification of growth centres;
- Critical evaluation of organizational support;
- Critical evaluation of the potential for industrial development;
- Identification of the pilot projects and of potential industries;
- Programming for the establishment of pilot projects.

Design and concept of the pilot projects

Pilot projects are designed to include:

- The establishment of appropriate developmental facility as the nucleus activity of the project;

- The setting up of identified industrial activities through the encouragement of private entrepreneurship by providing all necessary assistance and support.

Three pilot projects are to be identified for the respective development of agro-industries, marine product processing industries and handicrafts.

Pilot project components and potential industries

A pilot project in agro-processing – for example an agro-based products and process development (APPD) unit – should cover the following main functions:

- Research and analysis (of economic data for determining agro-industry potential);
- Product and process development (for promotion of industrial activities and for training and demonstration);
- Analysis and testing (of selected commercial products);
- Standardization and quality control (for manufactured goods);
- Industrial extension, liaison and coordination (for promoting an overall and integrated development of agro-based industries in the area and within the RRD region).

Considerations for the identification of potential industries

The base line for the identification of project activities (including the identification of potential industries) in the Delta must be the entailed impact on stimulating the development of the industrial structure. The government policy for promoting industrialization, as outlined in *The Socio-Economic Stabilization and Development Strategy to the Year 2000* is aimed at *(a)* encouraging industrialization alongside agricultural development and a priority to basic industries, supporting industries and agro-industries, and *(b)* fostering the development of processing industries in rural areas by accelerating the provision of various infrastructural facilities in these areas. The strategies to be adopted for the present purpose include the establishment of agro-processing industries, export-oriented industries and small-scale industries offering sound prospects for employment generation.

The basic criteria to be adopted for identifying industries holding a potential for development are the following:

- The proposed manufacturing activities should be based on the existing and potential resource endowments and demands of the area in particular, and of the region in general.
- They should be technically and economically viable on a small/medium-scale operation.
- They should have a quick take-off period.
- They should be based on relatively low-cost and simple technology, and tailored to the skills either readily available in the Delta, or within reasonable reach.
- They should be capable of stimulating growth in a number of related industries via forward/backward linkages.
- Activities utilizing waste and byproducts of agriculture and agro-industries, hitherto not utilized to any appreciable extent, merit special consideration.

In short, the objective here is to identify industrial activities that may act as catalysts for a rapid industrialization of the Delta through diversification of the present industrial activity, and based on a combination of skills, talents and technologies that are available or could be quickly generated to bring about a fast disseminating effect.

Possible growth centres and locations

The survey mission will have to identify three suitable locations (one location by province) for each of the pilot projects to be identified. With its strong agricultural base, Hai Hung province looks, *a priori*, suitable for the location of the agro-based product and process development unit (possibly at Haiduong city). The Handicraft Development unit could be based in Nam Ha province (Namdinh city), where handicraft skills are well developed and where there is potential for development of these industries. Thai Binh province could provide the suitable location for the Marine Product Development unit, as its production of fish products (shrimps from ponds in reclaimed land and fish from estuaries and off-shore grounds) is increasing.

Organizational set-up of the pilot project

The survey mission will make recommendations on the organizational set-up of the proposed pilot projects, their functions and linkages.

Notes

1. According to *Viet Nam Economic News*, No. 49, vol. IV, 9–15 December 1994.
2. Lall (1990 and 1994).
3. Lall (1990).
4. Ibid.
5. Ibid.
6. Ibid.
7. Lall (1994).
8. Lall (1990).
9. Such survey missions were undertaken in several ESCAP countries to plan for the establishment of pilot projects in selected non-metropolitan areas in Bangladesh, India, Indonesia, Malaysia, Philippines, Sri Lanka and Thailand.

12. Concluding Remarks

The methodology followed here is applied to a specific subset of Viet Nam, but can be readily transposed to cover the entire national territory. Indeed, apart from region-specific recommendations such as those relating to the infrastructure layout, most of the elements of the suggested action programme hint at an improvement of the policy, regulatory and institutional environment and therefore encompass a broader, countrywide coverage.

To some extent, the same analysis when conducted at the national level should be somewhat easier inasmuch as it would save the labour-intensive job of compiling ad hoc statistical aggregates. It would probably be more meaningful as its policy implications would be geared across the board to the whole economy, and would not entail potential distortions when, in effect, restricted to a particular region.

A more elaborate treatment would call for an in-depth analysis of the competitiveness of the manufacturing lines, at ISIC three-, possibly four-digit level of disaggregation. As manufacturing statistics in the country do not yet comply with the international system, this task alone would no doubt prove time consuming. In the process, however, the relevant authorities should be advised to adopt the ISIC format, as a next step in the standardization process that in 1993 saw the United Nations system of national accounts replace the former material product system in macroeconomic statistics.

The analysis would highlight the determinant of, and the constraints to, industrial competitiveness in the country. It must rely on standard quantitative tools to account for the actual complexity of manufacturing processes. A study on effective rates of protection would document the perverse effects of the present tariffs; a simplified computable general equilibrium model would, for instance, illustrate how, by distorting relative prices, the impact of such tariffs trickle down to the rest of the economy. An input–output analysis reflects intra- and inter-sectoral linkages and indicates, *inter alia,* the multiplier effects of investment flows; social accounting matrices are particularly useful when attempting to measure and monitor income distribution and the incidence of poverty in the country.

But more important perhaps than strictly technical considerations is the considerable effort the responsible government authorities will have to commit in the years to come, in order to strengthen their capacities in line with the requirements of their new role in a market economy. It will need in particular to build up a sharp expertise in modern industrial economics, a discipline that is sorely lacking in transition economies.

Bibliography (for Part II)

Binnie & Partners, Snowy Mountains Engineering Corporation Ltd, AACM International Pty Ltd, Delft Hydraulics (1993), 'Red River Delta Master Plan – Draft Master Plan', Ministry of Science, Technology and Environment, Hanoi, December.

_____ (1993), 'Red River Delta Master Plan – Development Options and Projects', Ministry of Science, Technology and Environment, Hanoi, December.

_____ (1994), 'Red River Delta Master Plan – Background Report No. 26: Village crafts: Development Options and Projects', Ministry of Science, Technology and Environment, Hanoi, May.

_____ (1994), 'Red River Delta Master Plan – Progress Report No. 7', Ministry of Science, Technology and Environment, Hanoi, December.

Economist Intelligence Unit:

Viet Nam Country Profile 1993/1994.

Viet Nam Country Reports 93–IV, 94–I, 94–II, 94–III.

Business Asia – Various issues in 1994.

Engineering Consulting Firms Association (1994), *Socialist Republic of Viet Nam: Basic Study Report on Industrial Development,* Tokyo, Japan, March.

Enos, J. and W. H. Park (1987), *The Adaptation and Diffusion of Imported Technology in the Case of Korea,* Croom Helm, London.

International Bank for Reconstruction and Development (1994), 'Viet Nam: Financial Sector Review – An Agenda for Financial Sector Development', Washington, D.C, 20 July.

_____ (1994), 'Viet Nam: Public Sector Management and Private Sector Incentives', Washington, D.C, 26 September.

International Labour Organization (1992), *Viet Nam: effects of government policies on the incentive to invest,* report prepared by David H. D. Truong.

Lall, Sanjaya (1990), 'Building Industrial Competitiveness in Developing Countries', OECD, Paris.

Lall, Sanjaya (1994), 'Technological Development, Technology Impacts and Industrial Strategy: A Review of the Issues', *Industry and Development* No. 34.

Mitsui, Hisaaki (1992), 'Effects of the recent industrial reforms in Viet Nam: A remarkable transformation to a market economy?', International Development Centre of Japan, Staff Occasional Note No. 3, March.

Mitsui & Co, Ltd. (1993), 'Master Plan for Basic Industry Development in Socialist Republic of Viet Nam', Executive Summary (Draft Final), November.

Ministry of Science, Technology and Environment, Government of Viet Nam – Core Counterpart Team on Industry (1994), 'Industrial Development Orientation in the Red River Delta to the Year 2010', MOSTE, July.

____ (1994), Background papers (in Vietnamese) on sectoral plans for heavy industries:

* building materials
  - chemicals
  - coal and gas
  - electronics
  - mechanical engineering
  - metallurgy
* light industries
* agro-processing

Socialist Republic of Viet Nam (1992), *Vietnam's Industrial Statistics (1986–1991): Allocation, Structure, Scale and Efficiency*, Statistical Publishing House, Hanoi.

____ (1993), *The international symposium on the transition to a market economy*, Hanoi, March. Proceedings of the symposium organized in November 1992 by the State Planning Committee with the assistance of the Economic Planning Agency, Japan, and of the National Institute for Research Advancement, Japan.

____ (1993), *List of licensed projects from 1988 to 1992*, SCCI, Ho Chi Minh City.

____ (1993), *Export Processing Zones and Industrial Estates: Investment Opportunities in Viet Nam*, State Planning Committee, Hanoi.

____ (1994), *Statistical Yearbook 1993*, General Statistical Office, Statistical Publishing House, Hanoi.

____ (1994), *The State Committee for Cooperation and Investment*, SCCI, Hanoi, January.

____ (1994), *List of licensed projects in 1994*, SCCI, Ho Chi Minh City.

United Nations Development Programme (1992), 'Red River Delta Master Plan – Project Document', Hanoi, October.

____ (1994), 'Red River Delta Master Plan – Minutes of the first Tri-Partite Review Meeting', Hanoi, 18 March.

____ (1994), 'Red River Delta Master Plan – Report of the Joint Evaluation Mission', Hanoi, June.

____ (1994), 'Briefing Note on the Socialist Republic of Viet Nam', Hanoi, July.

____ (1994), *Viet Nam Technical Assistance in Transition*, Hanoi, October.

____ (1994), 'Red River Delta Master Plan – Project Profile', Hanoi, 20 December.

United Nations Economic and Social Commission for Asia and the Pacific (1991), 'Regional Study on Promoting International Competitiveness and Efficient Resource Utilization in Manufacturing in Asia and the Pacific', Bangkok, December.

_____ (1993), 'Promoting International Competitiveness and Efficient Resource Utilization in Manufacturing: Case-studies of China, Viet Nam, Lao People's Democratic Republic and Mongolia', New York.

United Nations Industrial Development Organization (1987), 'The Republic of Korea: Commercialization of Research and Development Results with Particular Reference to the Small and Medium Industry Sector', Regional and Country Studies Branch, PPD.21.

_____ (1993), 'Industrial Restructuring and Industrial Policy in Vietnam', Jürgen Reinhardt, in *Viet Nam's Dilemma and Options: the Challenge of Economic Transition in the 1990s*, Mya Than and Joseph L.H. Tan (Eds), Asean Economic Research Unit, Institute of South-East Asian Studies, Singapore, pp. 76–96.

_____ (1993), 'Micro-level Industrial Policy in Sri Lanka (SRL/91/031) – The Cascading Tariffs Trap', Occasional Research Paper, Jim Robertson.

_____ (1994), 'Industrial Cooperation for Promotion of Investment Projects in Developing Countries (GLO/92/185) – Investment Promotion Report, with Special Reference to the North and South Triangle Zones in Viet Nam', Vienna, February.

_____ (1995), 'Advisory Support to the Export Processing Zones Programme of Viet Nam (VIE/93/801)', Tom Kelleher, Arthur Kavanagh and Stellan Cyon, January.

Viet Nam Investment Review, several issues in 1994–1995.

Appendix 3. Tables to Part II

Table A.1   Industrial employment by source of ownership (1,000 workers)

	1985	1990	1991	1992	1993
Total	26,020.3	30,294.5	30,974.2	31,818.9	32,716.3
Industry	2,800.1	3,392.0	3,394.0	3,450.0	3,521.8
Industry as % of total	10.8	11.2	11.0	10.8	10.8
1992 breakdown					
State (total)				694.7	
State (central)				405.6	
State (local)				280.7	
Non-State				2,755.3	

Source: Statistical Yearbook 1993, General Statistical Office, 1994.

Table A.2   Yearly growth of industry by source of ownership, in real terms (Percentages)

	1986	1987	1988	1989	1990	1991	1992	1993
GDP*							8.6	8.1
Industry	6.2	10.0	14.3	–3.3	3.1	10.4	17.1	12.1
of which:								
State (total)	6.2	9.3	15.5	–2.5	6.1	11.8	20.6	13.3
State (central)	5.6	6.8	12.3	5.9	15.3	15.5	23.1	14.1
State (local)	7.1	13.0	19.9	–13.5	–8.9	4.2	11.5	10.0
Non-State (total)	6.2	10.9	12.9	–4.3	–0.7	7.4	9.6	9.0
Cooperative	14.8	5.8	1.0	–36.1	–20.0	–41.6	–31.1	–2.3
Private	–6.5	19.9	31.8	34.5	10.4	26.7	16.9	10.2

Source: Statistical Yearbook 1993, General Statistical Office, 1994.
*Not available before 1992 – System of National Accounts replaced Material Product System in 1993 and GDP figures were officially reconstructed for 1991 and 1992 only.

Table A.3 Contribution of major industries to gross output in 1992: breakdown by source of ownership
(Billion dong, at 1989 constant prices)

| | Total | State | | | Non-State | | | |
		Total	Central	Local	Total	Cooperative	Private	Household
Total manufacturing*	13,992.6	8,661.1	5,054.9	3,606.0	5,331.7	513.1	513.3	4,305.3
Food; Foodstuffs	6,140.3	3,845.0	1,853.0	1,992.0	2,294.9	101.6	127.1	2,066.6
Textiles; Sewing products	1,685.2	1,111.6	781.4	330.2	573.6	98.5	149.2	325.9
Construction materials	1,383.5	902.4	706.8	195.6	481.1	64.8	28.4	387.9
Chemicals	1,355.2	1,009.4	632.9	376.5	345.8	53.8	24.3	267.7
Equipment and machinery	668.1	352.3	222.0	130.3	315.8	37.8	9.3	268.7
Wood and wood products	610.9	140.8	40.1	100.7	470.1	46.1	59.2	364.8
Electric and electronic products	300.3	220.0	170.8	49.2	80.3	12.2	7.8	60.3

Source: Statistical Yearbook 1993, General Statistical Office, 1994 – UNIDO calculations.
* = Total industry minus electricity and fuels, to adjust GSO definition.

Table A.4   *Contribution of the industrial sector in the RRD to gross output in 1992: breakdown of gross industrial output by province and by source of ownership*
(Billion dong, at constant 1989 prices)

	Total	State	Non-State
Total country*	8,962.2	3,624.2	5,338.0
Red River Delta**	1,369.8	538.5	831.3
of which:			
Ha Noi	389.3	221.6	167.7
Hai Phong	151.4	89.6	61.8
Ha Tay	161.9	26.7	135.2
Hai Hung	11.4	18.6	92.8
Thai Binh	122.7	38.2	84.5
Nam Ha	172.9	53.9	119.0
Ninh Binh	45.2	16.3	28.9
Quang Ninh	72.5	42.1	30.4
Vinh Phu	89.3	28.1	61.2
Ha Bac	53.2	3.4	49.8

Source: Statistical Yearbook 1993, General Statistical Office, 1994 – UNIDO calculations.
*Excludes Central State's industrial output.
**According to definition of RRD Master Plan project, i.e. GSO definition + Quang Ninh, Vinh Phu and Ha Bac.

Table A.5   *Number of industrial establishments by source of ownership*

	1985	1986	1987	1988	1989	1990	1991	1992
State (total)	3,050	3,141	3,157	3,111	3,020	2,762	2,599	2,268
State (central)	711	687	682	681	666	589	546	537
State (local)	2,339	2,454	2,475	2,430	2,354	2,173	2,053	1,731
Non-State								
Cooperative	35,629	37,649	33,962	32,034	21,901	13,086	8,829	5,723
Private	920	567	490	318	1,248	770	959	1,114
Private households	0	0	0	318,557	333,337	376,900	446,771	368,000

Source: Statistical Yearbook 1993, General Statistical Office, 1994.

Table A.6   Number of industrial establishments in 1992: breakdown by province and by source of ownership

	State			Non-State		
	Total	*Central*	*Local*	*Cooperative*	*Private*	*Household*
Total country	2,268	537	1,731	5,723	1,114	368,000
Red River Delta* of which:	809	265	544	2,620	132	139,872
Ha Noi	253	142	111	1,031	37	11,161
Hai Phong	101	21	80	283	49	6,010
Ha Tay	63	14	49	323	9	43,751
Hai Hung	47	17	30	149	2	18,326
Thai Binh	52	1	51	184	4	27,310
Nam Ha	88	10	78	288	7	6,585
Ninh Binh	42	4	38	16	5	1,119
Quang Ninh	50	14	36	122	0	6,083
Vinh Phu	75	29	46	99	7	12,263
Ha Bac	38	13	25	125	12	7,264

Source: Statistical Yearbook 1993, General Statistical Office, 1994 – UNIDO calculations.
*According to definition of RRD Master Plan project, i.e. GSO definition + Quang Ninh, Vinh Phu and Ha Bac.

Table A.7   Number of State industrial establishments in 1992: breakdown by level of employment

Total	*<100*	*100–500*	*501–1,000*	*1,001–3,000*	*3,001–5,000*	*>5,000*
2,271	873	1,117	165	94	12	10

Source: Statistical Yearbook 1993, General Statistical Office, 1994.

Table A.8 Investment in 1992: breakdown by origin
(Billion dong, at current prices)

	Total investment	State investment				Non-State investment	
		Total	Central	Local	of which RRD*	Total	of which household
Total investment	18,431	7,566	4,956	2,610	658	10,864	9,419
Per capita total investment (dong)	265,552	109,018	71,411	37,607	34,992	156,534	135,713
Investment in industry	5,097	3,643	3,133	510	n.a.	1,455	n.a.
Per capita industrial investment (dong)	73,443	52,483	45,138	7,345	n.a.	20,960	n.a.

Source: Statistical Yearbook 1993, General Statistical Office, 1994 – UNIDO calculations.
Note: GDP is 110,535 billion dong to which industry contributes 23,956 billion dong.
*According to definition of RRD Master Plan project, i.e. GSO definition + Quang Ninh, Vinh Phu and Ha Bac.

Table A.9 Average output per industrial establishment and per worker in 1992: breakdown by source of ownership

	Gross output*	Number of establishments	Number of workers	Number of workers/ establishments	Output per establishment**	Output per worker**
Total country	8,962.2	377,105	3,450,000	9.1	23,765.8	2,597.7
State	3,624.2	2,268	694,700	306.3	1,597,971.8	5,216.9
Non-State	5,338.0	374,837	2,755,300	7.4	14,240.9	1,937.4
Total Red River Delta***	1,369.8	143,433	n.a.		9,550.1	
State	538.5	809	n.a.		665,636.6	
Non-State	831.3	142,624	n.a.		5,828.6	

Source: Statistical Yearbook 1993, General Statistical Office, 1994 – UNIDO calculations.
*Billion dong, at constant 1989 prices.
**Thousand dong, at constant 1989 prices.
***According to definition of RRD Master Plan project, i.e. GSO definition + Quang Ninh, Vinh Phu and Ha Bac.

Table A.10 Value of output by productive sector in the RRD in 1992
(Billion dong, at current prices)

	Total	Agriculture	Industry	Services	Others	Industry/ Total (%)
Red River Delta*	35,716.3	11,228.1	10,804.5	13,578.3	105.4	30.3
of which:						
Ha Noi	11,111.5	695.4	4,431.7	5,892.9	91.5	39.9
Hai Phong	4,927.3	944.4	1,553.3	2,426.4	3.2	31.5
Ha Tay	5,917.0	2,599.2	2,042.4	1,273.1	2.3	34.5
Hai Hung	4,005.9	1,861.4	805.7	1,335.6	3.2	20.1
Thai Binh	3,229.1	1,974.7	549.8	703.1	1.5	17.0
Nam Ha	4,975.3	2,445.0	1,040.1	1,487.9	2.3	20.9
Ninh Binh	1,550.2	708.0	381.5	459.3	1.4	24.6

Source: CCT on industry, RRD background report, 1994.
*GSO, seven-province definition.

Table A.11 Main industrial outputs in the RRD* in 1992

Products	Units	Total country	RRD	RRD/ country (%)
1. Electricity	million kWh	9,818.5	2,500.0	25.5
2. Steel	thousand tonnes	175.2	12.0	6.8
3. Soldering irons	thousand tonnes	1.1	1.0	90.9
4. Machine tools	thousand tonnes	884.0	884.0	100.0
5. Hydraulic pumps	thousand units	500.0	396.0	79.2
6. 'Lotus' tractor 12 CV	thousand units	600.0	600.0	100.0
7. Insecticide pumps	thousand units	52.7	52.7	100.0
8. Diesel engines	units	3,300.0	2,000.0	60.6
9. Electric rotating engines	units	12,900.0	10,531.0	81.6
10. Transformers	units	3,000.0	1,800.0	60.0
11. Electric fans	thousand units	257.0	216.5	84.2
12. Assembly of TVs	thousand units	1,040.0	565.0	54.3
13. Bicycles	thousand units	80.0	74.0	92.5
14. Chemical fertilizers	thousand tonnes	507.0	100.0	19.7
15. Chemical paints	thousand tonnes	4.3	2.5	58.1
16. Tubes and tyres for automobiles	thousand pairs	8.6	8.6	100.0
17. Standard battery	million units	68.0	30.0	44.1
18. Soldering sticks	tonnes	3,865.0	3,865.0	100.0
19. Detergents	thousand tonnes	66.5	16.0	24.1
20. Toothpaste	million units	15.3	3.0	19.6
21. Cement	thousand tonnes	3,727.0	1,353.0	36.3

Table A.11   (continued)

Products	Units	Total country	RRD	RRD/ country (%)
22. Lime	thousand tonnes	667.4	64.0	9.6
23. Stones	thousand m³	4,560.0	2,156.0	47.3
24. Paper, covers	thousand tonnes	111.6	5.1	4.6
25. Electric bulbs	thousand units	9,604.0	5,000.0	52.1
26. Thermos bottles	thousand units	661.0	661.0	100.0
27. Glass and glass products	thousand tonnes	32.3	8.1	25.1
28. Beer	million litres	162.1	47.0	29.0
29. Cigarettes	thousand packets	1,523.0	143.0	9.4
30. Textile fibres	thousand tonnes	42.5	10.1	23.8
31. Fabric of all kinds	million metres	175.7	54.0	30.7
32. Canvas	thousand metres	1,452.0	1,200.0	82.6
33. Mosquito nets	million metres	41.5	8.3	20.0
34. Hosiery	million units	17.7	9.0	50.8
35. Towels, handkerchiefs	million units	110.0	21.0	19.1
36. Ready-made garments	million units	63.9	12.0	18.8

Source: CCT on industry – RRD background report, 1994.
*GSO, seven-province definition.

Table A.12 Distribution of manufacturing value-added: breakdown by subsector
(Percentages)

ISIC subsector	Total country				RRD region*				Total country/RRD region*			
	1986	1990	1991	1992	1986	1990	1991	1992	1986	1990	1991	1992
31. Food	28.4	44.2	44.0	44.3	15.8	17.7	19.5	21.8	31.0	50.1	48.9	49.0
32. Textiles	17.9	13.6	12.6	12.6	26.5	27.3	23.5	20.0	16.2	10.5	10.5	11.0
33. Wood	9.0	5.0	4.9	4.1	5.2	5.9	6.2	6.7	9.8	4.8	4.6	3.6
34. Paper	4.2	3.6	3.3	3.3	3.0	2.3	2.0	2.5	4.5	3.9	3.5	3.5
35. Chemicals	10.3	8.0	9.1	9.9	10.3	7.2	7.2	8.4	10.2	8.2	9.5	10.2
36. Non-metal	9.3	10.0	11.0	11.0	13.9	18.1	21.5	21.1	8.4	8.3	8.9	8.9
37. Metal	1.5	1.9	2.6	2.9	0.4	0.1	0.6	0.3	1.7	2.3	3.0	3.5
38. Machinery	15.5	10.5	9.7	9.2	21.8	17.6	16.5	16.2	14.2	8.9	8.3	7.8
39. Others	3.8	3.1	2.8	2.6	3.1	3.7	3.0	3.0	4.0	3.0	2.8	2.5
TOTAL	100.0	100.0	100.0	100.0	100.0	100.0	100.0	100.0	100.0	100.0	100.0	100.0

Source: Statistical Yearbook 1993, General Statistical Office, 1994 – UNIDO calculations.
*GSO, seven-province definition.

Table A.13 FDI flows in manufacturing in 1988–1992 and 1993: breakdown by subsector (US$, at current prices)

	Total country						RRD region*					
	1988–1992			1993			1988–1992			1993		
ISIC subsector	US$	No. of proj.	Average $/project	US$	No. of proj.	Average $/project	US$	No. of proj.	Average $/project	US$	No. of proj.	Average $/project
31. Food	307,749,732	54	5,699,069	44,180,216	20	2,209,011	9,051,700	2	4,525,850	16,532,533	3	5,510,844
32. Textiles	125,154,620	38	3,293,543	304,652,467	29	10,505,257	15,226,800	3	5,075,600	5,210,667	5	1,042,133
33. Wood	77,441,143	34	2,277,681	14,927,914	12	1,243,993	1,376,650	2	688,325	8,769,400	3	2,923,133
34. Paper	44,920,000	7	6,417,143	17,794,000	7	2,542,000	4,400,000	1	4,400,000			
35. Chemicals	462,522,378	33	14,015,830	59,343,817	21	2,825,896	3,080,770	4	770,193	4,764,000	1	4,764,000
36. Non-metal	343,198,391	20	17,159,920	53,109,919	17	3,124,113	290,179,463	5	58,035,893	2,371,428	2	1,185,714
37. Metal												
38. Machinery	237,544,090	36	6,598,447	506,838,657	29	17,477,195	75,946,000	9	8,438,444	226,836,240	8	28,354,530
39. Others	25,699,987	18	1,427,777	23,067,200	14	1,647,657	3,000,000	3	1,000,000	4,800,000	4	1,200,000
TOTAL	1,624,230,341	240	6,767,626	1,023,914,190	149	6,871,907	402,261,383	29	13,871,082	269,284,268	26	10,357,087

Source: SCCI, list of licensed projects in 1988–1992, and in 1993 – UNIDO calculations.
*GSO, seven-province definition.
Note: Figures under the years 1988–1992 represent aggregates over the period.

Index

191

Printed and bound by CPI Group (UK) Ltd, Croydon, CR0 4YY

23/04/2025

14660975-0001